Commitment To Love

DEANNA McCLARY
with Jerry B. Jenkins

Commitment To Love

Thomas Nelson Publishers
Nashville

To my precious husband, Clebe,
whose loyalty, courage, strength, and commitment to love
motivate me to reach my fullest potential
as his wife and lifelong companion.
And to Tara and Christa,
the beautiful reflections of our love.

Published in Nashville, Tennessee, by Thomas Nelson, Inc. and distributed in Canada by Lawson Falle, Ltd., Cambridge, Ontario.

Printed in the United States of America.

Scripture quotations are from THE NEW KING JAMES VERSION of the Bible. Copyright © 1979, 1980, 1982, Thomas Nelson, Inc., Publishers.

ISBN 0-8407-7632-2

2 3 4 5 6—92 91 90

Contents

Foreword

Years ago the Clebe McClarys were in our home.

I was struck by Clebe's manliness. Every inch a marine, every inch a gentleman, every inch a Christian. I was aware that part of Clebe had been left behind in Vietnam. But what was left was so much more of a man than the average man one sees every day that he commanded not pity but respect. I knew Deanna was proud to be Clebe's wife, and he deserved her.

When I was asked to write a foreword to Deanna's book, I felt honored and was eager to read the book. Once I started it I could hardly put it down. Deanna's honesty is disarming and challenging. The picture we get of Deanna's and Clebe's backgrounds demonstrates the impact of strong family values, the warmth and security they provide. Deanna's commitment to Clebe illustrates beautifully that love is not merely emotion. Loving is doing. Love is a commitment. And as we live out commitment, love grows. Not automatically, but with good hard work, humor, and lots of forgiveness.

This is a great book for our time with so many marriages breaking up and so many people living together without benefit of marriage or commitment! I, for one, believe that there is a vast majority of grassroots Americans that simply don't go along with the secular view of morality. But even if we are in the minority, we know it is what God planned for marriage.

This book will inspire readers with ideas and incentive. Thank you, Deanna, for sharing your experiences with us. They will be a tremendous help to thousands of couples.

Mrs. Ruth Bell Graham

CHAPTER *1*
The Telegram

The day after my twentieth birthday, March 4, my attention was focused on seeing my husband again. Clebe and I had been married less than a year, and he'd been in Vietnam more than half that time. In a few days, he would be on his way to Hawaii for a week of rest and recuperation, and I would meet him there!

Everything I said or did pointed to that trip. I had never been far from Florence, South Carolina, and Hawaii sounded as exotic as the Orient. But seeing Clebe was most important. I had to touch him, to hold him, to be with him. From the day he had left, I had missed him so deeply that I ached.

I wasn't the only one who believed that Lieutenant Patrick Cleburn McClary III was the most handsome Marine, the perfect southern gentleman, and the best husband a girl could have. He was a favorite of both sides of our new family, an athletic man's man who sounded too good to be true only to those who hadn't met him.

Mother and I had parked in front of Shirley Meyer's beauty shop and were just walking through the door when I heard one of the beauticians call out, "If Deanna McClary is here, tell her she has a phone call."

I immediately turned to my mother.

"Something has happened to Clebe."

"Oh, Deanna! There's no reason to . . ."

But I knew. I don't know how, but I knew. It could have been anybody on that phone. I had lived in Florence most of my life and had many friends. But my eyes narrowed; my breathing was shallow; I felt a tightness in my chest as I headed for the phone. It was Aunt Estelle.

"Deanna, honey, you need to come home right now."

I didn't have to ask why.

"Is Clebe alive?"

"Deanna, there are two men here from the Marine Corps, and they aren't telling me anything. They have to talk to you in person."

Clebe was dead. What other news would be delivered in person? I dropped the phone and ran out to the car, Mother close behind.

"Let me drive, honey."

"Mother, please just get in the car!"

I should have let her drive. I could hardly see through my tears.

"He's dead! I know he's dead!"

"Honey, we don't know."

"I know he's dead."

I raced through town faster than I ever had. Our dreams, our plans, our hopes, were crushed. There was no question in my mind. He was gone. How could our storybook romance and marriage be over so soon? Even our first meeting on October 6 of 1965 had seemed providential. . . .

So many things had come together coincidentally when I met Clebe. I had returned from cheerleading practice, tired and disheveled, wearing saddle oxfords and plaid Bermudas.

My eighth-grade sister, Annette, had been outside waiting for me. "Dea, can you take me to the mall? A bunch of my friends are playing in a band there." Annette was a cheerleader at Moore Junior High in Florence, and several of her friends were playing at the opening of the new Florence Mall.

"Are you kidding? Look at me! I look like a teeny bopper. Forget it."

"Come on, Dea! I just need a ride. They're starting any minute. You don't even have to go in."

"Yes, I do! I haven't bought Mother's present yet. Run in and tell her where we're going."

It wasn't like me to do something on the spur of the moment like that. I didn't know it would be a momentous day. I just thought I would kill two birds with the same stone. She needed a ride. I had forgotten Mom's present. Forget the hair. Forget the outfit. We'd go.

As soon as we arrived at the Florence Mall, a boy in a Mustang convertible called Annette over. I didn't like that. I kept an eye on them as I parked, because I was protective of my little sister. I had dated enough to know what to watch out for, and I didn't want Annette getting the reputation of a girl who comes running when a boy calls. She waved me over as the boy got out of his car.

"Coach, I want you to meet my sister, Deanna. She's a cheerleader at the high school. Deanna, our coach."

I was stunned. This was no boy; this was one gorgeous man. He was thin and tanned and muscular, and he looked like a Greek statue. He wore sweat pants and a letter sweater, but still I wished I hadn't been wearing Bermudas and knee socks! The coach reached to shake my hand and introduced himself.

"Kleemucklarry."

That's what it sounded like to me, in his mumbled accent.

I was taken with his brilliant smile. *So this is the guy all my girl friends said I just had to see, the one they said was the most sought-after bachelor in South Carolina.* Annette and her friends had bubbled about him since the beginning of school.

"Larry?"

He was still smiling.

"Kleemucklarry."

I missed it again, but for the moment, I didn't care. He was the best-looking man I had ever seen. As we walked into the mall, I realized we would soon come into the atrium area where the band was to play, and maybe the coach would be embarrassed to be seen walking in with us. I turned to him and smiled.

"Well, it was sure nice to meet you."

And we walked off.

I found out later that he thought I was pretty stuck up to walk away after just meeting him.

He looked too young to be a teacher and coach at a junior high school. I didn't know he was seven years older than I was; I guessed he was just out of college, maybe twenty-two. As we crowded around to listen to the combo, I sneaked glances at him. Every time I did, it looked as if he were staring at me. I blushed. He smiled. Inwardly, I swooned. He was adorable.

Then I saw a girl on his arm. She seemed to look lovingly at him, and I thought she must be his girl.

A boy on our football team asked me if I had met the coach.

"Yes. What's his name?"

"Clebe McClary."

"Oh!"

"You want to go talk to him?"

Did I!

"He looks like he's with a date."

"No, that's just one of the player's sisters."

"Well, all right."

I found Clebe easy to talk to, even in the state I was in. I kidded him about showing off with all his letters and awards in basketball, football, and track on his sweater. He smiled.

"Aw, I just threw this on for somethin' to wear."

He was shy, and I sensed he was telling the truth. He seemed genuinely humble. I developed an instant crush, but I didn't think it showed. My goal was to keep it from Coach McClary, but it was transparent to everyone else.

When the band took a break, the coach excused himself to head back to school and grade papers. My face must have still been flushed. Annette and her girl friends surrounded me.

"Well? Well?"

I couldn't keep from grinning.

"Well . . . what?"

"How did you like him?"

"He was all right."

"All right! Did he ask you out?"

"Of course."

It was a lie. They bought it.

"Really? When?" They jumped and giggled, attracting more of their friends.

"Saturday night."

"Where?"

Some of them were shouting the news all over the place, so I knew I had to confess.

"I'm just kidding, y'all. Don't be ridiculous. He's too old for me. And anyway, there's no way he'd be interested in me."

When Annette and I got home that night, I realized I had forgotten to buy Mother's birthday present!

Now, as I rounded the corner of the driveway onto our street, I hung onto the picture of the strong, handsome Coach McClary.

I screeched to a stop behind the house and leaped from the car without turning off the engine. A Marine officer and a physician stood at the top of the steps on the back porch. I bounded up the stairs, sobbing. If I could get past these Marines, I wouldn't have to hear the news just yet.

The officer, Major Burleson, caught me by the shoulders and thrust his face close to mine. I could hardly breathe for the sobs racking my throat.

"Mrs. McClary! He's alive. He is alive!"

I had been so sure Clebe was dead that the panic and the grief had already begun. And now this! I looked from him to the doctor, who nodded. In an instant, I was calm.

"He's alive?"

The major led me into the house.

"He has been wounded, and he has suffered some serious injuries, but he *is* alive. I've been assigned to read you the telegram exactly as we received it, but bear in mind that the Marine Corps always makes these messages sound worse than they are. Hang on to the fact that he's alive."

The telegram was addressed to me at 2112–A Timmonsville Highway, Florence, South Carolina, and carried a "do not phone" instruction. It read,

---

A REPORT RECEIVED THIS HEADQUARTERS REVEALS THAT YOUR HUSBAND SECOND LIEUTENANT PATRICK C MCCLARY III SUSTAINED INJURIES ON 3 MARCH 1968 IN THE VICINITY OF QUANG NAM REPUBLIC OF VIETNAM FROM A HOSTILE GRENADE WHILE ON PATROL.

HE SUFFERED TRAUMATIC AMPUTATION OF THE LEFT ARM AND SUSTAINED SHRAPNEL WOUNDS TO ALL EXTREMITIES. PROGNOSIS POOR. OUTLOOK DIM.

YOUR GREAT ANXIETY IS UNDERSTOOD AND YOU ARE ASSURED THAT HE WILL RECEIVE THE BEST OF CARE. YOU SHALL BE KEPT INFORMED OF ALL SIGNIFICANT CHANGES IN HIS CONDITION.

I was numb. Clebe had been blown apart! The major explained that by "traumatic amputation," the Marine Corps meant he had lost his arm in combat, not later in surgery. The message had specified "hostile grenade" to differentiate it from an accident caused by a U. S. weapon. I was so relieved to know Clebe was alive that the severity of his injuries didn't even sink in.

My mother broke down at the news about Clebe's arm and the shrapnel wounds to all extremities. I couldn't make sense of everything. All I knew was that he was alive. I could live with any injury, any disability. I loved him and would be whatever he needed me to be. I didn't know what made me that way. I still don't.

I didn't realize that the telegram had been intended more to prepare me for Clebe's death than to reassure me. He was not expected to live. The words *prognosis poor, outlook dim* slid right past me, though I was a nurse-in-training. Had a doctor talked of a patient that way at the hospital, I would have known his condition was grave.

Now all I wanted to know was where Clebe was and how quickly I could get to him. The major knew Clebe was to be evacuated from Vietnam to the U. S. Army 249th General Hospital at Camp Drake, Osaka, Japan, but several phone calls to Washington ended in frustration. The major looked weary.

"He's not in Japan yet. At least he's not at the two-forty-ninth. But there's nothing to worry about. He's in transit somewhere."

After I had been so certain he was dead, no news other than that could be bad news. I know now that I was young and naive, but I believed that if I could get to Clebe, or they could get him to me, I could keep him safe, could get him back on his feet, could literally will him to survive.

The news of Clebe's being wounded somehow reached the Associated Press, and people all over Georgetown and Florence began to hear it on the radio. I called Clebe's mother where she worked, but when she answered, I was sobbing again. I barely managed to convey the message.

"Mother, Clebe has been seriously wounded."

She tried to calm me so I could tell her more, but the very thought of breaking that news to his own mother overwhelmed me.

"Clebe's been shot! Hurt badly. It doesn't look good. I've got to get to him!"

By the time she got home to the plantation where Clebe's dad was manager, several townspeople had arrived to console her. She asked one of the hands to find her husband.

"Tell Mr. Pat that Clebe's been seriously wounded and to come home quickly."

When Dad McClary got home, he wept openly for the first time in years.

I was relieved to learn through the State Department that Clebe had indeed finally arrived at the hospital in Japan. Though I was desperate to be with him and willing to spend every cent I had to get there, I was advised by the military to wait.

"There's too big a risk that he'll be coming home the same time you'll be heading over there."

Had I known the wait would be weeks, I wouldn't have allowed myself to be talked into staying in the States. Colonel Seth Dingle, a friend of the McClary family, was in Southeast Asia at the time and was asked to check on Clebe. His report was devastating. Clebe looked so bad that Colonel Dingle wouldn't even let his wife, Catherine, visit at first.

A few nights later Dad McClary called me with more news from Seth Dingle.

"Clebe lost an eye. It was completely blown out."

My in-laws didn't want to keep anything from me. They were convinced that I was a key to the healing of their only son. If I could get to him, knowing in advance the extent of his injuries, they believed I could help. I didn't say so at the time, but they were right. I just knew it.

Meanwhile, I was of help to Clebe's parents, visiting them as often as I could between classes and exams and spending weekends there. Mrs. McClary could do little but pace through the house, wringing her hands. I knew exactly what she was going through. It was the most difficult time of my life, waiting, not knowing anything for sure, praying and hoping that Clebe would live, that he would return.

I was frustrated beyond belief. In my mind my husband was a shell of his former self, depending on life-support systems half a world away. At times I thought I'd go crazy, waiting for some word. Fortunately, Major Julian Dusenbury, a friend who had been wounded in World War II, warned me to beware of crank calls by sick people who get morbid satisfaction from scaring victims. Sure enough, one evening a caller told me he was from the State Department in Washington and was sorry to inform me that my husband had died at 0900 hours.

I screamed for my mother. The line had gone dead, so she called Major Dusenbury, and he put our minds at ease.

"Someone would visit you if Clebe had died. And even if someone did call, he wouldn't hang up on you."

Still I felt as if I were falling apart. The waiting and the not knowing were tearing me up. One day, about two weeks after Clebe's injury, when I could stand it no longer I went to a back room of our house and dialed the operator.

"You have to help me."

I told her all about Clebe and where he was supposed to be. She was so sweet, it was as if she were an angel.

"I'll do what I can and call you back."

Several minutes later, the phone rang.

"Mrs. McClary? Hold for your party."

For my party? Could it be? Would I finally be able to hear Clebe's voice? To talk to him? All I had received from him since he'd been gone, besides dozens of letters, were several poor quality cassette tapes.

The static on the line was thick and heavy, but I could make out the sound of a receiver being moved about.

"Clebe! Clebe, honey! Is that you? It's Deanna!"

There was mumbling, but I couldn't make out the words. Still, there was no doubt it was Clebe.

"Darling! It's Deanna!"

Finally, I could understand that low, muffled, distinctive accent.

"Mother? Mother, is that you? I can't hear you!"

His voice broke, and I heard the phone drop. For the second time, I was convinced that Clebe was dead. Only this time, the worst horror of all: I had killed him! To satisfy my curiosity, my need to hear him, to express my love to him, I had killed him. Perhaps a blood clot had been dislodged, or some shrapnel had moved and sliced an artery. Why had I called? I was more convinced he was dead now than I had been when Aunt Estelle had first called.

I hadn't told anyone of my plans to call. Now I pleaded with my mother to get Dr. Bryant, a friend of the family, to try to reach a doctor in the hospital in Japan. I feared Clebe was lying there dead with the phone on the floor, and no one even knew it.

At least two hours passed before Dr. Bryant could get through to the hospital. When it was finally doctor speaking with doctor, we got some answers. Clebe was still alive, but his only remaining hand was taped next to his body. An orderly had set the phone up next to the ear that had suffered the worst damage. Seth Dingle had told him previously that his parents had called to ask about him, so Clebe assumed his mother was on the phone. In trying to shift the phone to his better ear, it had slipped. Someone came by and hung it up.

Finally, after all the waiting and frustration and fear, Dr. Bryant persuaded the doctor in Japan to put the phone up to Clebe's better ear. I was going to get to talk to my husband, to hear his voice, to assure him that I would always stand by him, no matter what. I held my breath.

"Clebe?"

"Yes, honey. I . . ."

"Oh, Clebe, I love you so much! I want to be there, but they tell me you'll be home soon."

His voice was muffled and weak from the trauma of his injuries, but that telltale, throaty accent still came through.

"Dea, honey, I'm so sorry. I messed up our Hawaii honeymoon. I'll make it up to you someday, and we'll go somewhere nice."

There he was, worried about our plans when I thought I had lost him. Even worse, I heard a pitiful sadness in his voice, almost a resignation. I'd never heard or seen anything like that in Clebe, and I didn't like it. I didn't think anything but death could weaken my husband's spirit, but I didn't know yet how close he had come to wishing he were dead.

Japanese protesters burned the American flag, threw

rocks through windows, and shouted "Yankee, go home!" If it hadn't been for the incredible coincidence that one of my high-school classmates, Stuart Simmons, was in the bed right next to Clebe's, I don't know how Clebe would have survived. Stuart read Clebe's mail to him, helped him write home every day, and generally served as his hands, arms, and ears during the weeks he spent at the 249th. Stuart himself had lost a leg.

Dr. Hunter Stokes, also a friend of Clebe's family, was an eye specialist assigned to another hospital in Japan. When he had heard about Clebe, he had made the long journey to see if he could be of help. He had examined Clebe, and assuming that Clebe was fully aware of the extent of his injuries, he had said something that shocked Clebe into a deeper depression.

"You know, the way they make artificial eyes these days, no one will ever know you lost an eye."

Clebe swallowed painfully. "Hunter, have I lost an eye?"

He'd thought it was just swollen shut and bandaged over like the rest of the left side of his face. It had been two weeks since he was wounded, and he had not been allowed a mirror. He told me years later that that was when he came the closest to wanting to end it all. He'd rather have died than to come back to me half a man, a shadow of his former self. His body burned with pain all over, his eye was gone, his arm was gone, his legs were ground like hamburger, and one was open and draining. One eardrum had been shattered beyond repair; the other would never be the same. The hand grenade that blew up in his face came after the satchel charges that had severed his arm. When he had covered his eyes, only his right hand remained to protect his face.

His face had been laid open from the forehead to the chin, directly through the center. His nose was ripped open ver-tically, his lips split, almost every tooth shattered. The hand on his remaining arm was so badly injured that doctors weren't sure they could save it at all.

As I gradually became aware of the details of each injury, I prepared myself for that day when the government would fly him into the States and I could once again be at his side.

I lived and died for every scrap of information any of us could obtain from the State Department, from our congressmen and senators, from Hunter Stokes, from Seth Dingle, from Clebe's daily letters, lovingly written by a Red Cross worker, and from Stuart, a friend from Florence. For several weeks no one knew exactly what city he would fly into after leaving Japan. I hoped and prayed it might be Charlotte or Columbia or even Florence—somewhere close to home, where both he and I would have some security.

We didn't know what his condition would be. I wanted him back so badly I could feel it, but I didn't want them to ship him out so soon that he wouldn't survive the trip. The more I heard about his wounds, the more curious I was about what had happened to him, when, where, and why. I wanted to hear about all of that only from Clebe, and only when he was ready to talk about it.

I continued spending weekends with Mr. Pat and Jessie McClary, leaving strict instructions with my family that any word about Clebe should be phoned to Friendfield Plantation immediately. To keep our sanity, Mrs. McClary and I pretended that every weekend would be the momentous one.

One weekend in early April of 1968, just about a month after Clebe was wounded, I was preparing a peach cobbler while Mrs. McClary was leaving for work. I made yet another hopeful prediction.

"You watch, Mammy. Just as soon as I get this in the oven, they'll call and tell us to come and see Clebe."

It was uncanny. A half-hour later, just as I closed the oven door, the phone rang. It was Senator Strom Thurmond's office. They had tried calling me in Florence and were told I was in Georgetown.

"Your husband is being flown out of Japan tonight on a medivac plane. It will land at Andrews Air Force Base in Maryland, and he should be at Bethesda Naval Hospital by tomorrow."

I was so excited I don't even remember saying good-bye. My hands shook as I dialed Mrs. McClary's office. She was home within minutes, phoning the airlines. She pleaded with them to hold the last three seats for Mr. Pat, herself, and me on a flight that was to leave Charleston for Washington in an hour and a half. We were ready; we had been packed for weeks. A few minutes later, while we were heading out the door, the airline called again.

"Don't rush. Your seats are reserved, and the plane is a couple of hours late."

That took some pressure off, but when the plane did leave, my head pounded with anticipation and the fear of yet another postponement. It was hard to believe the tedious wait was really almost over. The moment I had anguished over—to see and hold my husband—was near.

"Dear God, please don't let anything happen."

During the flight, I thought about the last time we had been at the Charleston airport. Clebe had been leaving for Nam. Few can imagine how vivid are the sad memories of that airport.

Mrs. McClary's sister and brother-in-law, Lucille and Dorsey Delavigne, picked us up at the airport in Washington and took us to their nearby home. We waited by the phone in their kitchen. Uncle Dorsey knew a man from the Pentagon who was stationed at Bethesda Naval Hospital and had a contact at Andrews Air Force Base. He promised to call as soon as Clebe's plane touched the ground. It was after ten that night when we got the word. Clebe had been transported on a stretcher from the plane to an ambulance. My heart ached for him. I should have known he would still be unable to walk, but news of the stretcher reminded me again of the severity of his injuries.

At midnight we received a call that Clebe had arrived at Bethesda Naval Hospital. I wanted to rush to his side. But there was another excruciating message: "He's exhausted from the trip. No visitors until morning."

I was crushed. I didn't think I could wait another minute. It was clear in Mom and Dad McClary's eyes that they felt the same. Had I been alone I would have broken down, but I wanted to be strong for Clebe's parents. I couldn't speak. I held my head high, took a shower, dressed, and sat on the couch. There would be no sleeping this night. I was ready to leave as early as Uncle Dorsey wanted.

The next morning Senator Strom Thurmond's office called to offer us a limousine and driver, but Mom McClary gratefully declined.

"If Clebe can have visitors, we're on our way."

CHAPTER 2

Seeing Clebe

Not many Marine Corps lieutenants are admitted to Bethesda Naval Hospital. It is intended for dignitaries, high-ranking officers, statesmen, and politicians. Of the hundreds of men flown from Japan to Washington via Alaska the night before, Clebe was the only one taken to Bethesda.

Probably due to the efforts of Senator Strom Thurmond, Clebe's admittance had been cleared, but there was no room for him. He spent half the night in a hallway, then several hours in a temporary station before being assigned to a double room on the fourteenth floor. All the McClarys and I knew on that interminable elevator ride was that Clebe was up there somewhere. When the doors opened, I was glad to see a group of doctors and nurses, because I knew one of them would be able to tell me where my husband was. But before I could ask, they recognized us and began talking, seemingly all at once.

"We need to prepare you for the way your son looks."

"We need to prepare you for what to say to your husband."

"Your reaction to how he looks is crucial to his psychological health and vital to his recovery."

"Let's sit down a moment and discuss . . ."

I had waited long enough.

"Just tell me where my husband is. I've had nurse's training, and I want to see him. I can take it. Talk to his parents if you must, but let me be the first to see him. Where is he? Please!"

Someone took me seriously.

"Last room at the end of the corridor."

I headed down that hall, heart pounding. At the end I saw a closed door on the right, what looked like a closed closet directly in front of me, and a door partially open to the left. That had to be it, and when I heard Clebe's muffled accent, I was certain. I didn't plan what to say. I knew I wouldn't be repulsed, no matter what. I imagined I would see him with a bandage over his left eye and one arm missing. I didn't worry that I would say the wrong thing or grimace or turn and run. Though everyone agreed that Clebe was ruggedly handsome with sparkling eyes and a huge grin that could get the attention of any girl he wanted, I had fallen in love with his spirit, his soul, his personality, his character. No hand grenade could damage that, and if it had, my job would be to put it back together.

I hesitated before the door. I could no longer hear Clebe's voice, yet it had come from this room, hadn't it? From my nursing experience, I was used to the smells. All that was left to overcome was my fear of the unknown. I pushed open the door, hoping I was in the right room. But I wasn't. The man on the left had both arms dangling and bandages everywhere else. I could see both his eyes.

The man before me had his head bandaged, one eye, and *no* arms! The part of his face I could see was clearly not Clebe's. I stared at the huge red-and-pink scars, the jagged stitches, the broken teeth and the lips so swollen that they turned inside out. Now what was I supposed to do? Their wounds didn't make me sick. I was full of pity and hurt deeply for them, but I didn't want them to think I was just standing there staring at them. Neither could I turn and walk out on them, for then they would think they had sickened me.

I was lost in time and space. I couldn't stay. I couldn't leave. They seemed to be looking at me, but maybe they hadn't seen me. I wanted to excuse myself, but words wouldn't come. I chose the lesser of two evils and tried to slip out as quickly as possible. Before I left, he spoke.

"Dea, honey, don't leave me. I know I'm not too pretty, but I thank God I'm alive to be with you."

I spun around. The emaciated man before me had my husband's voice. He was trying to smile, that jagged row of shattered teeth showing between the bloated lips. Stitches from his forehead to his chin held his scarred face together after several operations already performed in Japan. Looking more closely, I could see that he did have his right arm, but it was in a cast and bound tightly against his body. His remaining hand had been ripped apart by shrapnel, splitting open the fingers and tearing out the tendons, leaving them in a clump in his palm.

One leg looked like ground beef, the other was open to the bone from hip to foot, oozing, the muscles exposed, Clebe's slow, steady, strong heartbeat evident in the throbbing tissue. Some of his stitches were reinforced by metal staples, but bits of metal that I would later learn were shrapnel fragments glistened from nearly every inch of exposed skin.

The bandages around his ears left the top of his shaved head exposed. It was no wonder I hadn't recognized him. Anything and everything that physically represented Clebe before was now either gone, ravaged, sewn, or full of fragments. I ached for him, but I wasn't repelled. To me, he was beautiful because he was Clebe and he was home and he was mine. And I told him so. I rushed to him and carefully embraced him. I don't mind saying that I would have loved to climb right into that bed with him and press his body close to mine, but he was fragile and sensitive.

The muscle tone was gone, his weight down more than fifty pounds. He had assured me over and over in his letters that the pain wasn't bad, and now I knew the truth. If his body wasn't screaming in pain from all this, then he was doped up past all normal consciousness.

Clebe was a mess. I couldn't try to predict how long it would take for him to be functional again, let alone normal.

His torn-up face was caked with blood, dried blood filled his nose, scabs appeared on his lips. Doctors wouldn't promise he could keep both legs or whether he would ever walk again if he did keep them. The remaining hand was in doubt, too, though no one gave him much chance of using it if it survived.

There was no resemblance to the picture I held in my mind of the tanned, muscular Coach McClary, wearing sweat pants and a letter sweater. Yet his determination, his inner strength, and his integrity were still there, I knew. I just had to help Clebe regain his physical strength. Together we'd show the doctors.

I stood back and shared my husband with his parents, content and happy to be with him at last. As I studied his thin frame with its various swollen parts trying to heal, I tried to picture what he would be like in a few months. He had already endured a half dozen operations, but I didn't know I would sit in waiting rooms or pace corridors through two dozen more.

His parents reacted as well as could have been expected. I know they were horrified and heartsick when they saw the shattered body of the healthy son they had seen leave for Vietnam. Mr. Pat had always called Clebe the finest example of manhood he had ever seen. Many people shared that view. Dad McClary had taught Clebe to hunt and fish and survive in the wilds from the time he could walk. That kind of childhood on Friendfield Plantation made Clebe an outstanding man, a respected leader of men, and a proficient lieutenant in the jungle.

Now as his parents shyly stood before his bed, he had to speak first again.

"I know I'm not much to look at, but I'm glad I'm back here with y'all."

His mother had resolved not to break into tears. She was cheerful and encouraging, though she told me later that if I had not been the first to go in, she wasn't sure she could have handled it. Clebe's father fought his emotions the whole way. To see his strapping son lying broken and nearly wasted away was almost too much for him. He stared at the seared face, the scabs, the remaining eye with no eyelid, no lashes, no eyebrow, and he fought to keep his lips from quivering.

Clearly, Mr. Pat felt helpless, and he wanted to do something, anything, for his son. He didn't want to have waited this long—harboring the terrible news and longing to see Clebe—and then just stand there and pity him.

"Son, is there anything we can do for you? Anything?"

Clebe tried to smile through those grotesque lips and the jagged stubs of teeth. "I'll tell you, Daddy, I sure could use a bath."

That was all Dad McClary needed to hear. He rounded up some corpsmen, and they set about the arduous task of getting Clebe from the bed to the bathroom and into a shallow tub. It was perilous to his worst leg, so they had to keep that out of the water. (Every few days they would have to dig and scrape the dead skin away, causing Clebe his greatest pain, but eventually that would pay off when the leg healed, scarred but strong.)

Clebe thought his daddy, of all people, would be strong enough to give him a bath, but it almost killed Mr. Pat. He thought he'd been prepared for anything, but this was too much. The smell of war was still on the man, the gunpowder, the dead skin, the rotting flesh, the infection, the blood. It's a wonder any of us were able to bear it.

At one point Mr. Pat staggered out of the bathroom and nearly broke down.

"Jessie, his buttocks have been nearly blown off. His back was blown up. His legs are blown up. There's hardly a part of him that isn't scarred and bleeding. That water is full of metal; you can imagine what's still in his body. I don't see how he'll manage on his own. He's as helpless as a little baby. He can't even wipe himself."

After the family saw that Clebe really was alive, their fear shifted to what I might do. They knew I loved him; they knew I was loyal. But could any woman be expected to stand for this? It wasn't Clebe's fault, of course, but it was not what I bargained for when I agreed to marry him. Would I quit now because I had been delivered damaged goods? No one but I knew.

Dear John letters devastated Clebe's wounded friends on every side. Why should his wife be any different? Personnel in military hospitals told of wives and lovers huddling with their families, trying to see their husbands and boy friends from a distance, then turning without even a good-bye, never to be seen or heard from again. (Statistics showed that between 60 and 80 percent of the wives of the severely wounded left their men, sometimes after seeing them once.) It wasn't entirely the women's fault, of course. Some of the men came back so bitter, so full of self-pity, that they drove their loved ones away.

I hoped Clebe didn't even wonder if I would leave him. I think he knew me well enough to know where my heart was. If he didn't, I tried to assure him with that first visit. I told him I would stay with his aunt and uncle, Lucille and Dorsey, if they'd have me. And I would be there for him every day when he woke up. I would do everything for him that hospital personnel would let me.

Years later some family members revealed their early fears. They hoped and prayed I would stay with Clebe because they could see how he responded to me. They knew my faithful love was the key to his rehabilitation.

I didn't stay just because it was the right thing to do. I wasn't a martyr, certainly not a hero. How could staying with the man I loved put me in *his* category, a true hero who sacrificed his body and risked his life for his country?

I didn't stay only because he needed me, though it was clear that he did. I loved being needed, finally, but I wouldn't have chosen what we both had to go through just so I could love the feeling.

I didn't stay because I was afraid of what people would say if I left.

I didn't stay because I enjoyed the functions of my role. I did them with joy because I felt necessary. No one could actually enjoy everything that goes into total physical care.

I didn't stay for any hope of recognition or glory. In the

years since the toughest time, many people have expressed envy at my ministry or lifestyle or marriage to a handsome hero. They have no idea what goes on behind the scenes, what we've been through, what we still sacrifice for the sake of a public ministry. Those who long for and pray for the same "opportunities" should thank God every day that they don't have to pay the same price. The fact is that I would not choose a public ministry; the cost is too great. The payoff might be worth it for someone who basks in the limelight; but for the person who would rather be in the background, the glare of the spotlight can be excruciating, whether anyone believes it or not.

I didn't stay because God told me to, because I wasn't even a Christian at that time. Had He promised that if I stuck with Clebe He would give him a ministry beyond our wildest imagination, a chance to share Christ with people of all ages and walks of life all over the country, it would not have motivated me. That's not where my heart was.

I didn't stay because Clebe begged me to. Although his voice had that tinge of self-pity, and I did hurt and ache and feel for him, I did not want to pity him. I could not have tolerated his feeling sorry for himself. The last thing I wanted was a sulking, pity-party type, sitting around our house for the rest of our lives, a bitter parasite who grew only more remorseful for the services everyone rendered him.

The fact is, I knew almost from the beginning that the man I saw in that hospital bed was the man I had fallen in love with. I never dreamed of leaving. Leaving wasn't an option. It wasn't even a fleeting thought. From the moment that first phone call came until today, my only thought has been that Clebe is the only man I have ever loved. For some reason, even before I had a mature spiritual bone in my body, I had the feeling that the more he needed me, the more I could prove my love for him. Inside, he was the same unscarred man I had married. Scars and injuries don't have to change a person.

I wanted Clebe to be a fighter, not like so many others who had given up, lost the will to live, and died. I wanted

Clebe to return to that voice of authority and assurance and confidence. Yes, he was badly wounded externally; I could handle that. But I cringed at the possibility that Clebe was wounded more deeply, in his spirit, where—like others—the disease of bitterness would eat away at him and eventually all those who loved him.

I didn't want him to feel useless and pathetic. I wanted him to be the leader, not a follower. I didn't want him apologizing for what had happened; rather, I wanted him to accept it and go on, never quitting, making the best of it.

The day would come when I would leave him standing outside the car in the rain, insisting that he open the door and get in himself. The day would come when I would let him struggle to keep peas and carrots on his fork because to continue to spoon-feed him would retard, rather than speed, his recovery. This was most difficult for me, but also most necessary. Nothing was more important to either of us than his regaining his independence.

But to tell you why I stayed in spite of all odds, that I cannot do. I can't even claim any virtue in it because it was not something I battled with and won. For some reason, leaving was always out of the question. Perhaps by knowing more about me and our love story, you'll discover something about commitment that even I can't articulate.

Even if the reason for fulfilling my commitment is never any clearer to you than it is to me, perhaps my story will make some of the struggles in your life and marriage more bearable. In this day of quick fixes, speedy divorces, instant answers to life's most difficult questions, my prayer is that something here might inspire you to press on regardless. It's the tough choice, the careful solution, the lengthy, agonizing struggle, that produces the most beautiful results. Sometimes it seems like a blind investment, having no idea of the return for your effort. Yet somehow you believe that one day, God will work everything out for His glory.

CHAPTER 3

Little Miss Robin Hood

$\mathcal{D}$addy says he named me Carol Deanna after the singer Deanna Durbin, but I know the truth: I was named after him and Mother, Dean and Caroline. I was sixteen months older than my brother, Dean, four years older than Annette, and eight years older than our baby sister, Jennie.

We should have had an idyllic childhood. We were very family oriented, and Daddy was always a wonderful provider. We had just about whatever we needed and wanted, and our house—for most of my childhood—was on a ten-acre plot in Florence, South Carolina. Just across the property lived Daddy's parents, Arthur Bartley Fowler, Sr., (whom we called Paw Paw) and Jennie Craver Fowler (whom we called Goggie). Less than forty miles away was the farm of my mother's parents, Clarence and Evelyn Willis, whom we called Pa-Pa and Ma-Ma.

To be part of a big, bustling family and be that close to grandparents on both sides—not to mention that Paw Paw was a railroad engineer and Pa-Pa was a farmer—offered us fun opportunities that few children enjoy. Being an engineer when Paw Paw worked was akin to being an airline pilot today; he was an engineer for fifty-two years. We were as proud of him and his responsible position as he was. He carried his six-foot-two frame with an air of dignity that befit his station in life.

At night we'd hear a certain whistle blow in the distance,

and that meant Paw Paw's train was returning from its regular trip to Savannah. We'd all pile into the car and go to the station. There would be Paw Paw, waving at us with one hand while the other elbow hung out the window of that big locomotive engine. His Atlantic Coastline friends called him Mr. Rollerbearing, because he was the one with the experience, the one called on to engineer the latest specialty engines.

Paw Paw had a permanent limp. He had suffered a broken hip during a fire that trapped him in the cab of the locomotive engine. Only the heroic efforts of a black fireman, who pulled him from the wreckage, saved his life. That left an indelible impression on Paw Paw and Goggie. In a time and in an area where bigotry and racism festered, my grandparents went out of their way to be generous, helpful, and kind to their black friends.

My earliest memories are of Goggie's boarding house on Cheves Street in Florence, South Carolina. That rambling white house was home to many unique and special people who became my instant friends. The boarders were like family. We used to play croquet and other games together on the front lawn, and, I believe, they helped shape the social part of the person I am today. I've never been intimidated by older people, and I never knew a stranger. Even as a tiny youngster, I wasn't afraid to run right up to the newcomers and get acquainted. They had been so many places, seen so many things, done so many things.

Miss Jane Hemingway had been to Hawaii and brought back grass skirts. She taught us to make leis from flowers. Imagine the hilarity when I tried to teach Dean, Jr., to do the hula!

There was music galore in that house. Many of the boarders played instruments, and it seemed everyone listened to records or the radio. I learned to sing all the popular songs of the day at Goggie's place.

I'll never forget the love-boat quality of that big home, always full of activity. I still smell the aroma of the tangy, acidic juice that filled the air when Goggie peeled oranges for me in the kitchen. The boarders would bring her bags of fruit, and Goggie would let me eat all I wanted.

My earliest impression of my father was as a great provider and an effective protector. He provided everything we needed or wanted, and he also watched out for us.

One day when I was in first grade, I was waiting outside the school for my ride home when a man drove up and called to me.

"Come here! I want to ask you something! I have some candy for you!"

My parents had been open in communicating with us about taking candy from strangers. I panicked and flew back into that school, wishing my daddy could be there to protect me. The school secretary called him, and for several days he came by the school early and watched for the stranger, who never returned.

It's painful to put this into print, because Daddy has come back to the Lord and hasn't had a drink in more than thirteen years. In fact, when we want advice, a sympathetic ear, we run to Daddy. But during my childhood, that was not the case. We respect him and admire him and love him now. But in spite of what a nice guy he could be, he was mean and unpredictable when he was drunk. Sober, he was an engaging, entertaining, eager-to-please, creative genius who could plan or build or sell anything.

I know I'm not the first child of an alcoholic parent, and I know that in the long run, good has come from bad. I believe it was my role as first-born that made me feel as if I were the protector of the other three when Daddy was in a rage. Somehow the dread, the panic, the embarrassment, made me more sensitive than I might otherwise have been. I found myself drawn toward the hurting children in my classes as early as the third grade, even before Daddy's drinking got too far out of hand.

I didn't understand it or even think about it at the time, but I was a sort of schoolgirl Robin Hood. Goggie and her big house served as a refuge from the turmoil at home, but I also wanted to be someone else's angel, a provider, a protector. At school I met one little girl from a large, poor family. She smelled, she was unkempt, and she dressed in rags. There was a quiet dignity about her in spite of all that, even though she was teased by some of the kids. My heart went out to her, and I didn't even know why.

Maybe it was because I saw myself in her. Even though I was always well-groomed and well-dressed, inside I felt pitiful and ugly. I believed truth came out of a drunk man's mouth, that the liquor made him say what he really thought. So when Daddy, whom I loved, said I was ugly or stupid, I believed him. When he sobered up and was nice to me, I didn't trust him.

"Honey, I'm so sorry for what I said. You're a nice, beautiful little girl, and I love you."

Lies, I decided. *All lies.*

One day after my parents had given me a beautiful birthday party with lots of friends and neighbors and relatives, I thought about that little girl from my class. I got a big box and put in it one of my new frilly dresses, some socks with lace, some powder and bubble bath, snap beads, and whatever else I could think of that was new and pretty. I tied a ribbon around the box and took it to school, hiding it under my coat and waiting for the right time.

During recess I sought out my third-grade teacher, Miss Jordan.

"Would you see that she gets this box but doesn't know who gave it to her? Just tell her it's from someone who likes her a lot and thinks she's special and wants to give her some things."

Years later that teacher reminded me of that incident and said it had prompted her to begin coaching the class on proper grooming, how to clean our nails and fix our hair, reminding us that anyone can look nice, regardless how old their clothes are. She really made a difference in that girl's life, and I'd like to think I did, too. I'd give anything to know where she is today.

If I had any Christian motives for such charity, they had

to come from Pa-Pa and Ma-Ma Willis. Pa-Pa kept his Bible by his easy chair in the living room of the farmhouse, and he and Ma-Ma read from it every day. On that farm I was free. The wonderful smells of that place are still in my memories after more than thirty years.

I was Pa-Pa Willis's first granddaughter, and because I was a girl, he thought I could do no wrong. He was a stern disciplinarian, quick to whip off his belt and spank his grandsons if they got into mischief, but to him, I was the greatest little girl who ever walked the face of the earth. He always asked Mother and Daddy if I could come spend some time on the farm. Most summers I spent a couple of weeks there.

I slept in a deep, soft bed in that cool, quiet country air that carried only occasional animal sounds. At four in the morning I would hear Pa-Pa eating breakfast and then driving off in the pickup to round up the hired help for a day in the tobacco fields. After he dropped them all off and came back into the farmhouse, Ma-Ma plopped a chunk of fresh, home-churned butter into a frying pan, and from my bed I smelled it sizzling. In my mind's eye I saw her sawing two huge hunks of homemade bread from a loaf and deftly soaking them in that delicious sizzling butter.

Then came the slices of real cheese and the flipping of that big grilled cheese sandwich in the skillet. I loved that bed, but I couldn't wait to get up. I knew it would just be a few seconds before Ma-Ma would call me.

"Deanna, honey, your breakfast is ready!"

I padded down to the kitchen where Pa-Pa sat watching me eat my daily grilled cheese sandwich and drink a huge mug of coffee, which was mostly sweet cream and sugar (like a warm milkshake). I sat there sleepy-eyed, wondering if heaven could be any better.

I was so proud of Pa-Pa. He was a college graduate and taught agriculture at a local technical school during the winter. He called me his farm girl.

"Okay, Farm Girl, we got to get out in the field. You're gettin' a little lazy on me here."

He lifted me high into the pickup and shut the door, then

drove down the road toward the barns. They were right there on his property, but to me, it seemed like a long drive. I loved it. I loved him. I loved life when I was away from home and in the country.

Usually I didn't like my hands to be dirty or dusty or muddy or sticky, but in the tobacco fields I didn't mind. The black girls could crop and tie tobacco so fast that I wanted to do it just like them. They laughed and laughed at my left-handed attempts. Even though I never got it right, I enjoyed the feeling of my gummy fingers sticking together.

After a day in the fields, I would play in the rows of corn in the back yard. They were so high that you could get lost in them and had to find your way out by looking up and remembering the cloud patterns. What fun it was, with the sweet smell of fresh tobacco and corn wafting through the hot summer air! Catching a whiff of similar smells today will carry me back there in a second, just like the smell of butter melting in a skillet reminds me of those farm breakfasts.

God and Jesus were friends of Pa-Pa and Ma-Ma. I never doubted that. Their quiet, almost casual references to the Lord made a deep impression on me. There was no wondering involved, no questioning, no doubting. Perhaps there had been at one time, but they had settled into a lifestyle in which God was welcome and necessary and vital, and He was as real to them as I was. I felt the same way about Him, especially when I was with them, but also when I was at home. Though I didn't know what salvation was, I assumed God was part of my life, and I believe He was active in my life long before I really understood what it meant to be a Christian.

That limited, innocent faith carried me through a lot of tough times over the next several years. The more Daddy drank and the more predictable his unpredictability became, the more I relied on my secret prayer life. By predictable, I mean that Daddy was basically a monthly drunk. I can say honestly that I could have endured physical abuse and would have preferred it over the verbal. He could make me feel so worthless and useless that I was left mentally crawling in search of self-esteem.

Relatives and people at church and school and in the neighborhood began telling me that I was pretty when I was still a little girl. I didn't understand it; I couldn't understand it. It didn't reach me, didn't get close to the core of my being. I didn't know it then, though it's popularly accepted psychological truth now, but my self-image, my self-worth, my entire sense of self, was completely wrapped up in what I believed my father thought of me.

Even though I went on to model, cheerlead, and compete in beauty contests, I was never satisfied with my looks. I became obsessed with trying to do the best with what I had, not because I thought I looked so great, but because I thought the only thing people responded positively to was my clothes or makeup or how I did my hair.

Over the years I've met countless "beautiful" women who have faced the same self-doubt and lack of self-worth specifically in the area of their looks. Although I don't fully understand it myself, I know it's true. Yes, attractive women eventually learn that others find them beautiful, but no, that fact rarely convinces them that they are beautiful. That little girl way down deep still believes what she was told as an impressionable child. It must be like the overweight person who loses a hundred pounds and sees a skinny body in the mirror and hears the accolades of friends, only to remain feeling like a fat person who has lost weight rather than like a normal-sized person.

Lack of self-worth is not the only complication that arises from growing up in the home of an alcoholic. Fear is a major result. As I look back on my life, it seems I was always afraid. Afraid things wouldn't turn out the way we planned. Afraid every social activity would end in embarrassment. Afraid Daddy's mood would change.

We had one of the most beautiful summer homes on Crescent Beach, which Daddy built himself. It was fantastic, and it represented the fun that Daddy liked to have. But alcohol possessed him to such a degree that he just couldn't go without the weekend's ending in disaster.

As much fun as it was to go down to the beach, I dreaded

it. The first day or so might be perfect. If Daddy wasn't drinking, he was as sweet and gentle as a lamb, loving, cheerful, outgoing, and fun-loving. But the moment I saw him with a can of beer, I wanted to escape. I knew what was coming. I would pray and hope and believe with all my heart that this time he would be able to stop at one beer. But it never happened.

Often Mother bucked up to Daddy when he was drunk and verbally abusive. Instead of letting him have his say and sleep it off, she challenged him, argued with him, got him more enraged. It wasn't her fault. No one knows how to deal with a drunk, and he was then incited even more.

We pleaded with Mother to leave every time Daddy got abusive, but she'd rather stand and fight. I felt like a child referee. I tried in every way to appease him, to talk him down, but it was no use. There was no reasoning with him; no one could do anything right.

We always survived; that's how I saw it. Despite all we went through, we must have been special to God, because He brought us through. Nighttime was the worst because we never knew what the darkness held. But if we could hang on until morning, Daddy would be sleeping it off, hung over, repentant, and quiet. I wanted God to help me make it through the night. At times I actually prayed that God would take my daddy away. I blamed our unhappiness on him.

We children developed a cancerous, bitter hatred toward Daddy that took a lifetime to overcome and heal. I realized my role. I was a protector. I was a mediator. I could cover my own terror and turmoil by being the buffer for my brother and sisters. I didn't know I was being prepared for different kinds of tough times ahead.

CHAPTER 4

Looking for Mr. Right

*F*ortunately, my grandparents on both sides were good models of spouses. Pa-Pa and Ma-Ma Willis never said a cross word to each other in front of us kids. I'm sure they had their disagreements and maybe they even argued. If they did, it was behind closed doors, and they maintained the image of being one in mind and spirit.

Paw Paw and Goggie squabbled now and then, but they never went to bed angry. He called her Shinny the Mule, because she was stubborn. But whether they'd fussed or argued or nagged each other earlier, every night he came to her before going to bed.

"Well, Shinny, give me a kiss good night."

They kissed each other, and he shuffled off to bed, falling asleep listening to Johnny Cash sing railroad songs.

Paw Paw encouraged me in my interest in medicine. Because of his hip injury, he had spent a lot of time in the hospital and endured considerable pain. Even when I was a little girl, I massaged his legs to make him feel better after he had worked a full day in his garden. And he always praised me for having a special touch, saying, "You're the greatest little nurse I've ever had."

From the time I can remember, I had been interested in mixing concoctions to make people feel better. I wanted to heal people, to take care of them.

One morning Mother complained of a painful lump in her throat that not even the doctor had been able to diagnose. It was like a cyst. I went to the kitchen and prayed that God would help me mix up something to cure her. I don't know what I was thinking of, but my motives were purer than my logic. I had enough sense not to put any cleanser or detergent in my "medicine," but I did add just about everything else. Baking soda, garlic, Alka-Seltzer, Worcestershire sauce, Texas Pete (tabasco sauce), salt, and a little sugar mixed with water to make a fizzy, bubbly drink that Mother dutifully drank while I silently prayed.

"Lord, please let this be the cure she needs."

It worked! Whether it was the salt or the Alka-Seltzer, I don't know, but Mother called the doctor and reported, "I don't understand it, but it went away."

That was such an encouragement to me that for years I dreamed of becoming a doctor. Mother encouraged me by giving me a microscope and a home chemistry kit. Paw Paw unknowingly encouraged me by prescribing Grove's Chill Tonic for whatever ailed me. Someone on the railroad must have gotten him interested in it, because he was totally sold. I got the impression that he was almost glad when one of us came down with some sort of chill, because that gave him the opportunity to pull out the Grove's, shake it up, and force a tablespoon into our mouths. It tasted horrible and I hated it, but I was also fascinated by it. Maybe it was only a placebo, and maybe it cured only a psychosomatic chill, but it worked. I had no idea what was in it, but it appeared to be little metallic particles that became evenly distributed in the white, gooey, gummylike, syrupy liquid when the bottle was shaken. It was the weirdest stuff I've ever tasted. (That's the way medicine was back then, the worst! Nowadays it tastes so good they have to put childproof caps on it!)

Bad as that stuff was, I wish I'd had some of it to prescribe for my other granddad. Pa-Pa Willis was diagnosed as having asthma and an enlarged heart. I had spent a couple of weeks there that summer, and my cousins and my brother and sisters and I visited him the first week of December.

When we got back to Florence, several of us sat on the floorboard of the back seat of our car—my brother, Dean, and our cousin, J. B. (James Braxton Lovett, my mother's twin sister Gee-Gee's son), were there—and prayed about something special we could get Pa-Pa for Christmas. We finally decided to pool our money, sell a few things, get our parents to chip in, and buy him a pig—as if he needed another one. Already people were telling him to slow down and quit doing so much work with the animals.

A week later, December 15, 1959, I was playing in the house when the phone rang. My mother answered it.

"Oh, no! Oh, please, God! No! Not my daddy!"

It horrified me. I had heard Mother yell at Daddy, but I had never heard her grieving like this. I ran to her.

"Mama! Mama! Everything will be all right!"

"My daddy's dead! A heart attack! Oh, God, no!"

I couldn't relate to death. No one close to me had ever died. I kept trying to tell her that everything would be okay, but she had been a daddy's girl, and she felt nothing would ever be okay again. Pa-Pa Willis had moseyed down to the creek to feed the ducks. When he didn't return for dinner, Ma-Ma got worried and sent someone to find him. They discovered him on his back in the shallow water, the bill of his cap sticking up. He had died of a heart attack.

I was deeply impressed by the way Ma-Ma handled it. At first she wondered aloud how she would carry on without her husband.

"We were like one."

But she held up well and strong. I was amazed by her faith. While everyone else fell apart, she was a rock. She grieved and she mourned and she was wounded, but she stood tall.

I knew they had been inseparable. Even at eleven, I associated Ma-Ma's strength with the fact that she was the one who frequently read the Bible, prayed often, encouraged the grandchildren to trust the Lord in everything. She said she believed that one day we would all be together again in heaven. That's when I knew that her faith was not just something she talked about. It was not just something she practiced to make herself feel better. It worked.

Seeing how my parents reacted to and obeyed and respected their parents made me want to respect authority. I even obeyed my father when he was the most unreasonable. He might forbid some perfectly good activity while he was drunk, and I obeyed. Maybe not cheerfully, but I did what he and Mother said, no matter what, even though many of my childhood dreams were blocked.

I had loved to sing for as long as I could remember, and as a family we often gathered around the piano and sang. We sounded pretty good on tape—with my brother, Dean, announcing—but we rarely performed in public. Mother was the only harmonizer or blender in our family. Everyone else wanted to be the lead singer, so we all sang the melody.

All that singing paid off, because, though I took six years of piano without ever really learning to play well, I was a standout in the school choirs. In junior high Miss Betty Ann Darby selected me as one of the Keynotes from the chorus, and we performed all over the state.

Mother saw more potential in me than I saw in myself, and she enrolled me in a local modeling school. She wanted me to gain poise and confidence, not realizing that she was fighting a losing battle against Daddy's influence on my life. He wasn't too excited about my modeling. Although I loved singing and enjoyed modeling, and though it gave me a certain ease in front of people, success never convinced me I was any better at the core than my daddy thought I was.

Through her position as a substitute nurse for Bernard Baruch, Aunt Gee-Gee made contact with Arthur Godfrey. My picture was sent to him, and he asked that I come to New York for an audition to be on his radio or television program. I was going to be there for a modeling session with *Teen* magazine anyway, so for a junior higher it seemed the break of a lifetime.

Daddy absolutely forbade it. Everyone begged and

pleaded with him to no avail. No matter what Mother or Gee-Gee or I said, it made no difference.

"Not my little girl!"

Maybe he was afraid I would leave home and never come back.

Maybe it was all for the best and I was protected from things I wouldn't have been able to handle, but at the time I didn't think it was so good. I thought Daddy had robbed me of my future. I was hurt, but I couldn't say much. I guarantee you I was going to do what he said.

I continued to sing, taking lessons from the top vocal coach of the area and then studying under a German professor who so intimidated me that I insisted my mother wait outside for me during my lessons with him.

By the time I was fifteen, I was uncomfortable around men because they reminded me so much of my father. I couldn't be myself. I was tense. I was nervous. There was no room for error. It seemed to me that excellence was the only standard.

I turned sixteen near the end of my sophomore year in high school and received permission from Daddy to help during the summer in the little country hospital where Aunt Gee-Gee was a nurse. I was supposed to be the receptionist, but if someone came in with a heart attack, I helped until Dr. Bryant arrived. I got excited about becoming a doctor and gained more confidence working with people and interacting with adults, including men. I was happy to hear Dr. Bryant and Aunt Gee-Gee brag on what they called my instinctive ability to deal with people's needs.

The problem was with boys my age. My background made me a little more sensitive and mature than most high schoolers, I think, because a lot of what my friends and their boy friends did and talked about seemed juvenile to me. I had a good time, and I dated several boys, but I seemed older than my dates, in judgment if not in years.

During the spring of my junior year, I was named to the

May Court, and we spent one long, hot day at school in all the activities. I hadn't had anything to eat or drink all day, so by the time my date and I went to a party that night, I was famished and thirsty.

"Would you mind finding me something cold to drink? I'm about dried out. Please. I'll take anything."

I meant a soft drink or lemonade or even water. Everyone knew I didn't drink alcohol. I had never touched the stuff. I knew I would be an alcoholic if I developed a taste for it. I binged on peanut butter and chocolate, just like my daddy did, so I figured I had the classic makeup for alcoholism. Alcohol so repulsed me and scared me that I was never tempted in the least to even try it. I was a teetotaler, and everybody who knew me at all knew that.

I still don't know what my date brought me, but it was tall and full and cold, and I downed it fast. I appreciated it so much; it felt like a cold stream in the middle of a desert. I had hardly thanked my date when I felt as if I were on fire from my throat to my toes. My head throbbed; my heart pounded. Suddenly I felt as if I weighed five thousand pounds and was about to crash to the floor. I was furious, but my friends thought it was hilarious.

"How much is two plus two, Dea? Where are you? *Who* are you? How many fingers am I holding up?"

I learned a hard, valuable lesson that both protected me and made me unduly suspicious as I grew older: you really can't trust even your friends to have your best interest at heart.

Near the end of that school year, in June of 1965, I sat at a lunch table chatting with my girl friends and looking at our copies of the new yearbook. It was a madhouse as students scurried to other tables to trade signatures and write messages.

At my table was a girl I had befriended because she was a loner. She belonged to a religion that did not allow women to shave their legs or show them in public. They were not to cut their hair. They didn't believe in going to doctors and dentists. As a result, she was very shy and very plain. She wore no makeup, had terrible teeth, and wore her hair in a long braid. Her skirts were ankle-length. I saw in her what I felt inside.

I spent a lot of time talking to her and walking with her. When I wasn't with her, she was alone. She was really a sweet girl, but few others took the time to find that out. She couldn't afford a yearbook, so she was looking at mine when he arrived at our table.

He was a wealthy boy, the kind who has everything he wants and needs and plenty that he doesn't. He had opened the yearbook to her picture and slid it under her nose.

"Loot at that!"

He threw back his head and roared with laughter.

"You're the ugliest thing! You're the ugliest girl in the book! Congratulations!"

Everyone was stunned to silence. He took the book back to his table where his friends snickered and he howled. I was enraged. For whatever bad had come from my life with an alcoholic father, much good had come from it, too. I had learned to stand up for myself and for others. I had learned what was right and what was wrong. I had a sense of justice, and from my dad, I had developed courage in the face of danger that would one day result in incredible actions. That day was just a foretaste.

I marched over to Mr. Cool's table.

"That's not fair! That's just not fair! Have you looked at your own picture in here, smarty pants? You're nothin' special yourself, you know. They wouldn't even put a picture in here of what you look like inside."

I was so incensed I didn't even listen to the catcalls he got for being told off by a girl. He was a big man on campus, but I was known, too. I was a cheerleader, a member of the May Court, a singer, a model. My point wasn't to humiliate him. I just wanted to protect the dignity and self-worth of a dear girl. Of course nothing I said or did about it took back the cruel words he had hurled at her.

Maybe I was wrong to fight fire with fire, but I'd like to think he never did anything like that again.

The Carol Deanna Fowler who began her senior year that fall at McClenaghan High School in Florence, South Carolina, was—as is typical of teen-agers, I guess—a jumble of parts. I had grown up in a big family where we had fun and we had plenty, but we also knew heartache and sorrow and pain and embarrassment. My brother and sisters and I were close and cared about one another, and we had been privileged—particularly the older ones—to have lived near and benefited from the counsel and protection of our grandparents.

I was a good student, and my teachers saw me as more mature than most of my contemporaries. I loved to talk to people, to draw them out, to get them to talk about themselves. I was sensitive to people's feelings and could usually tell when they had a problem or were hurting.

I enjoyed being popular and having friends, but inside I was scared and still saw myself as limited. Whenever anyone looked at me, I thought something was wrong with my makeup or I had a run in my hose. My dream of being a doctor went by the wayside when I learned how important science and math were to the profession. *I don't have to be a doctor,* I thought. *I can be a nurse.*

I was stunned years later to find that my sisters looked up to me and thought I had my act together back then. I felt so mismatched for life that I wouldn't have dreamed that anyone would look at me as a role model. Even as a fashion model, I felt like the awkward ugly duckling who had been encouraged to try so she could develop poise in spite of it all.

Though I dated a lot, I had picky things to say about almost every guy I dated. Either he wasn't chivalrous enough or he smoked or he drove crazily or I wasn't sure he didn't drink. I lay awake nights praying for a boy who would be the opposite of the way I saw my daddy. I was taller than most of my classmates, so I, of course, preferred tall, dark, and handsome men. But even more than that, I desperately wanted someone clean cut and all-American. I wanted no one short of Prince Charming.

I wanted a man special in every way. He should be strong

and smart and athletic and kind and gentle. He should be decisive and loving and responsible. I set my standards so high that no boy could hope to reach them, but I was too young and naive to see that. I wanted a knight on a white horse to rescue me, to give me a future that included living happily forever and ever in a kingdom far away.

I hadn't seen anything like that at McClenaghan High School, even though I had been voted into the very exclusive Sheiks Club, which anybody who was anybody belonged to. My daddy thought that was great. He remembered from his school days how important it was to be a Sheik—the high-school equivalent of a fraternity or sorority. Only I grew tired of it after awhile. As with most cliques, this was a club of exclusion. The members looked down on nonmembers, and many of my friends were excluded. I felt accepted but unhappy. There was always smoking and drinking, and I knew drinking led to unpredictability. The whole scene made me uncomfortable.

Everything that had gone into my life, the good and the bad, pushed me toward being a mature, responsible adult, and that was the kind of man I wanted, too. The potential at McClenaghan High looked a bit thin. I hadn't even considered an older man, until that day Annette needed a ride to the mall, and I met the man who would change my life forever.

CHAPTER 5

Trouble in Paradise

After that awkward meeting with Clebe at the mall that October day in 1965, I thought about him a lot. By Sunday afternoon I had convinced myself I was foolish to think I'd ever be able to date him. Then the phone rang. This time I understood him a little better.

"Deanna, this is Clebe McClary."

I panicked, but I tried not to let my voice show it. "Yes?"

"I met you over at the mall the other night."

I couldn't think of anything to say so I just muttered, "Oh?"

"Your sister introduced us. I'm the coach over at . . ."

"Oh, yes. Hi! Listen, let me switch phones."

That gave me a chance to talk to Mother.

"Mother, come here quickly! It's Coach McClary. What am I gonna do if he asks me for a date? What will Daddy think?"

She shrugged.

"A friend of mine says he's one of the finest Christian young men she's ever met, Dea."

I knew he had to be older to have gone through college and be a coach. Admittedly, he was well preserved, but I imagined he had to be an older man. I was petrified.

"Well, what if he asks me out?"

"It's fine, as long as we know where you're going."

I ran to the other phone.

"Sorry. I'm back."

"Yeah, uh, I was wonderin' if you'd be free to go to dinner and a movie with me tonight."

"Tonight? Oh, my, that's pretty late notice."

"I was gonna call you after church this mornin', but then I went scuba divin' and the time got away from me."

He was a churchgoer. That was good. And a scuba diver. That sounded impressive.

"I usually like to schedule dates a couple of weeks in advance."

"Oh, are you busy tonight?"

"Well, no, but . . ."

"I understand if it's just too short of notice. Maybe some other . . ."

"Just a minute, Coach. Let me check with my parents."

I covered the phone and could have screamed. I was not going to let this guy get away! To even be asked out by him was a special honor. One thing I for sure was not going to do was tell my daddy I was dating someone already out of college. I waited a few minutes, then picked up the phone again.

"I guess it will be all right, but I have to tell them where we'll be."

He said we'd be going to the Gang Plank and a movie and he'd pick me up at six. That gave me two hours to get ready, and I was going to use it all. An hour and a half later I was barefoot and in a bathrobe with my hair in curlers when Daddy asked if I'd run over to Goggie's and get his briefcase. I wanted to tell him there was nothing as important as my looking my best for this date, but he was in a bad mood. It would have been just like him to decide all of a sudden that I couldn't go out that night.

Clebe would be there in less than an hour, and I didn't want to get hot and sweaty running an errand. But rather than try to get out of it and risk Daddy's asking more questions, I dropped everything and flew out the back door. When he was in that mood and said jump, I jumped. I ran across the field to

Goggie's place, hoping the briefcase would be in plain sight so I could hurry back in time to put on my makeup.

I swung the back door wide open, hurried inside, located the briefcase, grabbed it, and sailed back out. In all my splendor—curlers, housecoat, bare feet, and no makeup—I ran into Clebe McClary on the porch. I was mortified. He grabbed me, and I trembled and tried to get away.

"Calm down, young lady!"

"Let me go! I've got to get dressed!"

I was horrified. He was smiling.

"Calm down! There's no hurry! I'm early because I wanted to make sure I could find your home. I've seen my sisters in hair curlers before."

I told him to go in and talk to my grandparents, then I ran home to finish getting ready. He still remembers the difference between how I looked on the porch and how I looked on the date. I hoped against hope he wouldn't mention it. He didn't. I was so nervous I could hardly talk. I was afraid my hands were cold and clammy, and what if he wanted to hold hands during the movie? Here I was with lots of experience dating boys my age, now out with a sophisticated man. I didn't know what to say or do, but I tried my best to be myself.

At dinner he asked if we could say the blessing.

"Sure."

I bowed my head and waited. And waited. Oh, no! Had he asked *me* to ask the blessing? Finally I looked up. There he sat with a big grin.

"Are you finished?"

I thought he'd meant he would pray aloud. He laughed, and I figured I'd blown it.

After that, everything was great. He held my hand at the movie, took me home on time, didn't try to kiss me, and promised to call me again. I didn't want to appear forward, but I told him I'd sure like to see him again.

We began dating regularly, and I learned a lot about Clebe McClary. He was obsessed with sports and his work, which also involved sports. He coached; he taught; he participated;

he officiated. He did everything. And everything he did, he did 100 percent. He never shirked a responsibility, never showed up late or left early. He did a job until it was done, and if that meant that our dates consisted of my driving his Mustang around the track, pulling a drag to smooth it out while he walked along behind to make sure everything was working, then that was our date.

Sometimes I spent time with him chalking a field or making signs for the gym. I would admit that I wanted to spend my time with him, he'd tell me all he had to do, and I'd let him know I was willing. Most girls would have thought he was crazy and might have been jealous of the time he devoted to his job and sports. I thought it was admirable. Some might have called him a workaholic. I knew better. He was committed. Whatever he did, he wanted done right, and he invested the hours to do it. I would have done anything to be near him. Often I just sat with him as he watched games on television. I was falling in love. Here was Mr. Right, a guy who was everything and more than I could have asked for.

During the week he sent Annette home with poems and notes for me, and on the weekends we were together constantly. I sensed he was shy about introducing me to his friends, because invariably they'd ask me what college I attended and I'd have to admit I was a high schooler.

Word got around that we were dating and before I knew it, the high-school principal called me in.

"Deanna, I've known you and your family for years, and I know you're a good girl. I also know Mr. McClary and have no doubt that he is a fine, upstanding young man. But you must understand that it doesn't look good for one of our coaches to be dating one of our students."

I didn't understand. What was he saying? That I looked easy? That our relationship couldn't be pure? But I never talked back to an adult, especially an authority figure. He continued.

"I'm not going to tell you that you can't continue seeing Coach McClary."

It's a good thing, because I wouldn't have been able to obey that rule.

"But I *am* going to ask you and Coach McClary not to be seen together a lot around town and that you not come as a couple to school-related functions. Understood?"

I nodded, but I was hurt. We obeyed, but it was painful to not be able to show to the world that we were dating, we were a couple, we were in love. At least I was. He had been engaged while a student at Erskine College, and when his friends started getting engaged, he thought that was the thing to do. His fiancée had pressed for more of his time and attention, but he had so much going that he didn't see marriage in his immediate future. She got mad and gave back his ring, which he immediately traded for a surf board, some scuba equipment, and a coat.

There was a lesson in that episode for me. I wasn't about to push. But it wasn't long before I knew I wanted to marry Clebe.

We weren't allowed to sit together or be seen together at school functions, so at the first basketball game that fall I wore a dime store diamond ring and told everybody Clebe had proposed. I was only kidding, of course, but when that got back to him, he wasn't amused.

"She must've got that out of a bubble gum machine. She didn't get it from me!"

I had hoped he would tell people that maybe someday we would be married, but I'm afraid the ring scam seemed a little too much like the rush he had gotten the first time around.

Still, come December, he was ready for a more serious commitment than even I was.

"This is my college ring, Deanna. Will you wear it?"

I was thrilled.

"You want to go steady with me?"

He nodded.

"I know it's asking a lot, because you'll miss all the parties and proms and everything, but I'd like us to go together."

Happy as I was to be asked, I wasn't sure. I had gone

steady for a few days once and felt uncomfortable. I was also thinking of the principal's advice.

"Clebe, I do love you, but I don't think I'm ready to isolate myself from my friends yet."

He'd already had a ring given back to him. He didn't want any more of that.

"Keep the ring. When you're ready, wear it and I'll know."

In a few weeks I counted the cost. Missing a few things that required dates was a small price to pay to go steady with the man I loved. I wore his ring. Soon he wanted me to meet his parents. I found the ten-thousand-acre Friendfield Plantation overwhelming. What a fantastic place for a boy to have grown up! His parents, Mr. Pat and Jessie, were wonderful and warm, and they welcomed me immediately. His dad gave me a big hug and started right in talking about hunting and fishing and life in the outdoors. I found him fascinating. I did wonder, though, what Clebe's parents thought of his dating a high-school senior.

A few days later, Clebe showed me part of a letter from his mother:

> We think Deanna is a fine girl. She is sensible, mature, and intelligent. Your dad especially likes her better than any other girl you have brought home, because she likes to talk hunting.

In truth, I hated hunting. Paw Paw Fowler had taken us hunting when we were children, and he would doze, urging us to wake him if we saw a deer. If I saw a deer, I tried to quietly shoo it away! I didn't like the idea of animals being killed. But to make a good impression on Clebe's parents, I showed interest. His dad—a dear man—made everything seem interesting. Later I would hunt with Clebe, hoping he would miss some of those shots and spare some creatures. (He rarely did.)

My family loved Clebe. He jogged five miles to see me in the morning before I left for school. After awhile, I started running with him. Of course, my mother's homemade breakfasts drew him to our place as much as I did, I'm sure. My sisters swooned over him; Dean, Jr., looked up to him; my parents were proud I was going with him; and he had Paw Paw and Goggie's unequivocal blessing. Goggie even sided with him when we argued!

Dating the most sought-after guy around and one who met my every desire for a man should have enhanced my self-confidence. All the activities I was involved in should have, too. I had lots of friends and gave the impression that I was together. Only I knew the secret. I was not together at all. Inside I was a scared rabbit. I felt useless, worthless, ugly, and stupid. In my head, I knew better. In my heart, I was convinced of the worst.

Clebe talked about his plans for the next year, and they didn't include me. He was going to coach a swim team at Myrtle Beach during the summer and then go in the fall to the University of South Carolina graduate school on a fellowship that would allow him to coach under the legendary Paul Dietzel. I dreamed of studying psychology on the same campus, but I was hesitant to look as if I were following him around. I wanted him to suggest it.

But he was getting short-tempered with me, a bit curt. Even my mother noticed. She wrote him, telling him she had seen a difference in how he treated me and suggesting that he tell me straight out if something was wrong. She said that all I ever seemed to do was to try to make him happy. Maybe I was coming on too strong. Maybe I was clinging. I don't know. He didn't say.

I know now that he was thinking about backing off and being sure of his feelings, because he could see that I had fallen for him. He had a lot of plans to carry out before he wanted to get married, but clearly I was thinking matrimony. Even though I knew enough not to mention it all the time—because I knew what his last fiancée had done—I couldn't hide my feelings.

When a local woman asked me to apply for the Miss Florence Pageant (which fed into the Miss South Carolina and Miss America pageants), I was thrilled. She thought I had a good chance of winning with my modeling poise and singing talent, and I began to dream that such an event would turn me inside out. If only I could win and be Miss Florence, I would be worthy of Clebe. He would see that I had something to offer. Daddy would see that he had been wrong about me. Maybe I would be able to change how I felt about myself.

I filled out the application and sent in the picture. Mother was thrilled. So was Aunt Gee-Gee. We all knew what Daddy would think, but this was something I had always dreamed of.

CHAPTER **6**

Facing Bad News

*W*hen I was asked to be a contestant in the Miss Florence pageant, I was nearly delirious.

I knew that Clebe would be thrilled, too. I couldn't wait to tell him. He'd be proud of me, happy he was dating a girl pretty enough to be selected for the pageant. I wanted him to think I was special, and I hoped that any success I might have—beyond being accepted—would make me feel better about myself, too. I had been told all my life that I was pretty and talented, but relaxing and enjoying that were beyond me. I didn't know why, but I thought the pageant might be the answer.

I wanted to see Clebe's big hazel eyes dance with pleasure when I told him. We sat in the front seat of his car, and a street light sparkled in his eyes. As I shared my wonderful news, his smile faded and he turned away. I was tempted to reach up and turn his face to me so I could see his reaction. But when he spoke, I was glad I hadn't.

"I hate beauty pageants. They're like hog shows."

"Clebe!"

"I'm surprised you'd even dream of such a thing! Up there parading around in a bathing suit in front of all those men! I don't like that at all. I'm not going to have anything to do with that."

"No! I *don't* like that part of it either. The rest of the

program is talent and interviews, and if I win, it means a scholarship and the Miss South Carolina Pageant. Miss South Carolina goes to Atlantic City for the Miss America Pageant. . . . I just want to win. I want to be Miss Florence."

"And you'll show off your body to do it!"

I was stunned. What was happening? I had noticed a change in Clebe since he had begun working weekends at Oliver's Lodge, where he would work for the summer. Maybe he had more time to think about our relationship and realized he didn't care for me as much anymore. Maybe he had met someone else. Maybe he just wanted time to think, to enjoy his freedom, to back off from a relationship that seemed to be heading for the altar.

I didn't want to think about any of that. All I knew was that my sweetheart seemed to be slipping away. The long gazes into each other's eyes, the lingering embraces, the sweet, gentle, sensitive conversations, were just memories now. I grew frantic and redoubled my efforts to hang on to him. Which, of course, only drove him away.

A few weeks before graduation and the Miss Florence Pageant, Clebe came out to the house for a date, and I knew something was wrong. Usually, he called me honey and darlin' and such. Not this time. He immediately suggested that we sit on the back steps so we could talk privately.

"Deanna, we need to talk. You know we have had a really great relationship. You're a very special girl."

Already my defenses were going up. I could tell what was coming, and I dreaded it.

"In fact, Dea, you're one of the most special girls I've ever met. We've had some great times together. There are no words to express how much you mean to me."

I wanted to interrupt him, to tell him I didn't want or need words. I wanted him; that was all.

"Your family is special, too, and y'all have fed me a lot of great meals. But it's real important for you right now to start thinkin' about your own future. You've got college comin' up, and with the problems you've had in your family, this is your opportunity to get out on your own and find out what you really want in life."

I tried to keep my composure, but I couldn't take any more.

"I know what I want in life, Clebe! I want you."

He ignored me.

"There are so many things I've done that you haven't experienced yet. You need to test your wings, get to know new people, go to college, date other people."

My world was collapsing.

"Is that what *you* want to do, Clebe? *You* want to date other people?"

"We both need to, Dea."

"I don't."

"Yes, you do, don't you see? It was unfair of me to go steady with you durin' your senior year. I see that now."

"I love you, Clebe. There's nobody else for me."

"There's nobody else for me either, Dea, but . . ."

"Yes, there is! I can tell. I know when you're being straight with me and when you're not."

"I'm just saying that we shouldn't be tied down to each other. We can still see each other, but see others, too."

I folded my arms and stood, moving away. Looking back over my shoulder, I settled wet eyes on him.

"I'm not for this, Clebe. I'm not for this at all. I love you with all my heart. I want to marry you. You go ahead and do what you want, date anybody you want, but there will never be anybody else for me. You're going to break my heart."

"I'll still see you, Dea."

"Well, I'll be here waiting."

"Dea, you haven't even lived yet, and I'm not ready to make a decision to be tied down the rest of my life . . ."

"Clebe, is it the pageant? If it is, I'll give that up. I'll do anything if we don't have to break up."

"No! Now, see, that's just what I mean. I don't want you to do something just because I say so. If it's somethin' you want to do, you should go ahead and do it."

"I won't if you don't want me to."

"Dea."

He turned to leave.

"Clebe, honey! Please don't do this to me!"

I cried, but he had made a decision. I lived and died for his promise that we would still see each other. I didn't want anyone to know I had lost him. When we were together, I acted as if we were still going steady. I didn't want word getting out that I was available, because no one else in the world interested me. I was convinced no one ever would.

Our dates were infrequent after that, and on each one I tried to win back his heart. I wanted him exclusively, and I looked for any sign that our old relationship had returned. I listened for my pet names, watched for that look, waited for that touch. I begged and pleaded and proved beyond doubt that I was as immature as he thought.

The final blow came one weekend, a couple of weeks before graduation. I didn't know it was to be our last date. In fact, when Clebe parked overlooking the Black River, I thought he was going to kiss me and all would be forgiven, forgotten, and returned to normal.

But he didn't. He looked straight ahead.

"You know, Dea, I think this is for the best. I'm starting a new position at USC. You've got four years ahead of you. You need to meet new people and . . ."

I turned and stared at his profile, then interrupted. "Clebe, I love you so much. I love you more than anything in the world. I just love you."

"Well, thanks. I 'preciate it."

I couldn't believe it! That's all I got for declaring my undying love—thanks, I appreciate it? I knew that it was the end.

"You don't love me? You can't say, 'I love you, too'?"

"Well, no. Right now, I can't."

That went through me like a sword.

"Well, then let's go. Take me home."

"Dea."

"Take me home."

I told Mother I didn't care if I ever saw him again. On the sly I wrote and pleaded with him not to tell too many people, because I wasn't telling anyone. I wanted no one to know. My family tried to make me feel better by taking my side against Clebe. Daddy was livid.

"If that boy ever sets foot in this house again, he'll wish he hadn't!"

I can't imagine a divorce hurting as badly as I hurt then. My life had been drained. All I had to look forward to was finishing high school and entering the Miss Florence Pageant. Clebe would be at graduation because he had helped out with the varsity football team, but he would not be there to see me, to share my moment, to wish me the best, to be my date, my life.

I turned my sights on the pageant with a vengeance. I wanted to win so badly that I threw myself into the medley my coach had prepared for me—"Getting to Know You," "I Enjoy Being a Girl," and "I Could Have Danced All Night." A live orchestra would accompany the soloists that night, and I couldn't wait. I got the most beautiful sequined sweet-sixteen dress I could afford, and I planned to totally give myself to the upcoming rehearsals. For my own sense of self-worth and to show Clebe McClary what he had given up, I wanted to be Miss Florence.

A week after graduation, Clebe showed up at our place in a brand-spanking new green Mustang. After having prayed that every phone call and letter would be from him, I was sure he had come to his senses, had realized he couldn't exist without me, and was there to plead with me to forgive him and take him back.

He had a small gift, which made my heart flutter. He hadn't given me a graduation present; there had been no reason. Maybe this was it!

"Is that for me?"

"Yeah. It's a graduation present from my mother."

I wished he hadn't come at all. If it hadn't been for the

upcoming pageant, I might have died of grief. I moped and mourned all day, continually telling my mother that I would never date anyone else.

"I never want to go through this again. It hurts too badly."

She told me I couldn't just sit around all the time and mourn.

"There are other Clebe McClarys out there, Dea."

"Mama, I don't think there'll ever be anybody like that again. I've never met anybody like him. Everybody else seems to drink, smoke, cuss, run around, act crazy. I can't believe this is happening. Why do things like this happen to me? I was so happy."

I wrote Clebe several letters, telling him I wanted him to be happy and that I wished one day we could get back together. "I hope you'll realize that I'm the one for you, because I realize you are the one for me."

He never answered those letters. I was more deeply hurt, and I grew angrier.

One afternoon I was at Goggie's house when the phone rang. It was Daddy.

"Dea! Get over here quick! It's your mama!"

Though wearing only a slip, I dropped the phone and flew out the back door and across the acreage. Rimming Goggie's property was a five-foot barbed wire fence that normally took a minute or two to maneuver through, carefully separating the strands and avoiding the barbs. I had built such a head of steam that I leaped that fence with room to spare.

As I dashed into the house, Daddy ran out. He tended to panic when anything happened to someone in the family. He pointed to her bedroom and hurried off, ashen-faced, to call an ambulance.

"There's something terribly wrong with her!"

I found Mother on her back on the bed, deathly still. I loosened her blouse and yanked it out from her skirt. Running through my mind was the fact that her daddy had died at age fifty-nine. I didn't know whether Mama was dead or alive, and

I had only seen artificial resuscitation demonstrated. I reacted instinctively and alternately pounded on her chest and breathed into her mouth. In a few moments, she came to.

We rushed her to the hospital and found she had an ulcerated colon. She would miss the pageant, but she would be okay. That's all that really mattered.

CHAPTER 7

Miss Florence

$\mathcal{T}$he afternoon of the Miss Florence competition I was at the beauty shop, getting my hair done the way beauty contestants did in the 1960s. The style wasn't flattering to my face, but it seemed important to follow the trends in such contests. Someone bold enough to stand out too much might draw interest or even respect, but she seldom won.

As I sat under the dryer, Aunt Gee-Gee strode in looking so much like her identical twin that it almost didn't register with me that Mama was in the hospital. Gee-Gee looked proud, almost mischievous.

"This just arrived from guess-who?"

She handed me an envelope and one long-stemmed rose. I couldn't imagine to whom she was referring. I instinctively touched the blossom to my face and breathed in its stunning fragrance. I set the rose in my lap and slit open the envelope. The message was simple.

"I'm counting on you to do your best in the pageant. Good Luck! Clebe."

I crumpled the envelope and note and set them, along with the rose, on the chair beside me. I assume they were swept away at the end of the day, along with the other waste.

That message brought me to an all-time low. I couldn't believe Clebe had the nerve to write that, let alone the nerve to send it. He had turned me into a despairing, angry young woman who had set her sights on winning the Miss Florence contest mainly to show him what he was giving up. I couldn't have been more cynical.

Yeah, sure! I'll bet you want me to win the pageant. You didn't even want me in it!

Now I wanted to win more than ever, just to get back at him. I wanted to hurt him as badly as he had hurt me; I was at a terrible point in my life. I had lost sight of the fact, though it's crystal clear in hindsight, that I was still helplessly in love with him.

It would have been difficult to be more motivated to win that night. First, I wanted to win for Mother. In spite of Daddy and his problems, she had encouraged me to go for what I wanted in life. She had sacrificed so I could learn to sing, to model, to achieve. She was so excited about my being in the pageant that I just knew winning it would bring joy to her life. It would ease some of her heartache and be the beginning of great things.

I also wanted to win for Aunt Gee-Gee, who had become a second mother to me. And for my brother and sisters. I felt responsible for them. I was their big sister. I didn't know till years later how they looked up to me, but I knew I loved them and would have done anything to make them happy.

I can't deny I wanted to win for me, too. So much was wrapped up in my winning that it was as if my total psychological health were at stake. I wouldn't have known that then, but I knew I had something to prove to myself. I believed that if a panel of judges said I was the prettiest, most talented, most worthy girl to be named Miss Florence, then *I* might finally believe it, too.

In reality, the timing of Clebe's note couldn't have been better for my sake. It made me so angry, so determined, that I was bolder during the competition than I had any right to be.

I hadn't been there for any of the rehearsals because of Mother's illness, so I was given a crash course in where to stand, when to come in with the orchestra, and how to do my part in the group choreography routines. I was shown how to use the microphone, but I had a delicious secret. A friend from high school wanted me to use a cordless mike he had designed. It could be clipped inconspicuously to my gown, and it would appear as if I weren't using a mike at all. It was programmed to work through the sound system, and I would be free to move about and gesture without worrying about holding anything.

I should have been scared to death in my first competition, but I loved everything about it from the opening minute. I was more than just unnaturally calm. I was ready. I had a purpose. A goal. I wasn't short of breath; I didn't tremble; my smile wasn't fake. I was confident, self-assured, going for it all.

I was glad the pageant started with the swimsuit competition. I knew if I could get through that without Daddy showing up and making a scene, the rest should be downhill. Though I had always felt flat-chested—for good reason—my suit flattered me, and I had been doing lots of exercises to define my figure, firm my thighs, and make me feel confident.

I had been sincere when I told Clebe that I liked this part of the competition least, but I knew how important it was. I hoped it was not just providing men an opportunity to gaze at a woman's body, but was an example of what young women could do for their bodies with discipline and work.

We had been at the beach so much that summer that I believed I was, if anything, too dark. The judges didn't think so, and I learned later that I had won the swimsuit competition. My height was to my advantage in the evening gown category, and I won that, too. It might have helped if I had known where I stood all along, but those announcements came later. On the other hand, I might have gotten overconfident.

I believe I was the first person in Florence to use a cordless mike, and it was the hit of the night. People buzzed about how I could be heard throughout the auditorium and was clearly communicating through the sound system, but they couldn't detect a microphone. The orchestra beautifully played the charts of my three-song medley, and I knew where to stand and how to move so the spotlight could keep up with me.

It was, however, as if I were two persons that night. One was this calm, confident singer who performed as if she were born to it, and the other was a silent observer, wondering where in the world she got the courage. It was as much fun as I have ever had, singing out clearly, really seeing and experiencing the audience, winning them over, working with the wonderful orchestra. The audience erupted.

I didn't win the talent competition because there were some fantastic performers. In fact, when I heard Valerie Bobbitt warm up backstage on the violin, I knew she had the talent crown in the bag. She played just as well before the audience, too. I was confident I had finished well and had at least not hurt my chances for the Miss Florence title. The question during the interview portion was something stupid about Batman and Robin—I said I preferred Superman—and I felt I handled it immaturely.

Only a local pageant holds its entire competition in one night. As the long evening drew to a close, the five finalists were announced. The winner would be Miss Florence and would represent the city in the Miss South Carolina Pageant. The runner-up would represent the winner if she could not carry out her duties for some reason. The other girls could attempt to qualify for the Miss South Carolina Pageant by competing in any one of several other contests during the next few months.

When I found myself on stage with four other girls, my courage was suddenly gone. I knew there was nothing left but the announcement. I couldn't change my standing if my smile faded or even if I fainted. It was all I could do to hide my racing heart. Every word echoed through my head. I wanted to win so badly it hurt. I wanted it for Mother. I wanted it for my brother and sisters. I wanted to show Clebe. I even wanted it for Daddy. But mostly I wanted it for me.

With a flourish of music and a drum roll, the fourth runner-up was announced. We held our breath. She bravely smiled and accepted her bouquet and prize. The rest of us stiffened even more. The same routine winnowed out the third runner-up.

That left Valerie Bobbitt, Judy Way, and me. The three of us held hands but were afraid to look at one another or say anything. I was convinced Valerie had won the talent competition with her magnificent violin solo, as good as any professional. And Judy, the daughter of a local doctor, was—in my opinion—the most beautiful girl in the pageant.

"And now, ladies and gentlemen! Second runner-up to Miss Florence in the 1966 pageant! Miss Judith Way!"

I breathed a huge sigh of relief, but then I tightened again. They had dragged out the first three announcements, but the next one couldn't be slow enough for me. I wanted time to plan how to deal with it. The last thing I wanted to hear right then was my own name. That would mean failure, defeat, humiliation. I would be ignored in the rush to congratulate the winner, whose name would not be heard in the din.

I held my breath and squeezed Valerie's hand tighter. If I heard her name, I would have won. I didn't want her to feel bad, but I knew her smile then would be the forced one of a courageous good sport, just as mine would be in the same circumstance.

"Ladies and gentlemen! The first runner-up to Miss Florence 1966, who will represent Miss Florence should she for any reason be unable to carry out her duties! Miss Deanna Fowler!"

Valerie burst into tears as the other contestants and I rushed to congratulate her. I was happy for Valerie. She was a beautiful, talented girl and would be a wonderful Miss Florence, but I wanted to cry, too. I felt defeated. I was so bankrupt in the self-image department that I couldn't see what I had achieved. I had won both the swimsuit and the evening gown competitions and had finished high in the talent area. I had finished second overall, beating out dozens of other contestants.

I accepted my bouquet and prize and kept that smile pasted on, but to me, that was just another disappointment, another setback, another failure. I was not the first runner-up to Miss Florence 1966, the second-place finisher in a major competition, a prestigious feeder into the Miss South Carolina and Miss America pageants. I was just little, old, ugly, worthless Deanna Fowler, a loser from the word *go*.

Perhaps if I hadn't put all my eggs in one basket, if I had simply hoped to be a finalist, I would have been thrilled. But to me, during that fragile time of my life, I saw only winning as acceptable. Anything short of that was losing.

One of the reasons for that sad attitude, I think, was that my mother used to try to encourage me by comparing me with everyone else. That can be as devastating as comparing yourself to yourself. I know that Mother had my best interests at heart and that she was trying to counterbalance Daddy's destructive comments. But she would say every day that I was beautiful. And if I didn't believe her or if I made some disparaging comment about myself, she would head for the comparison well.

"Look at that girl over there that everybody thinks is pretty. Do you think she's pretty? Well, so do I, but you know what? You're ten times prettier than she is. So if you think *she's* pretty, imagine how pretty *you* are."

That taught me to compare myself with everybody. I would catch myself walking into a room, checking out everybody else, and deciding who was best looking. I felt I was constantly being judged, reviewed, compared.

"Mother, please don't tell me I'm prettier than anybody else. I don't want to hear that."

I wouldn't have been able to articulate it at the time, but what I really wanted and needed was to be complimented on those character qualities for which I had some responsibility. Outside of having a talent in applying makeup, what right did I have to accept *any* credit for my looks? Besides the fact that I didn't believe people who thought I was pretty, beauty was a shallow thing to praise anyway. I needed praise for being loving or kind or helpful or a hard worker. Instead, I was confused, frustrated, and left unable to accept that even finishing second in a beauty contest was tremendous.

Many people crowded around to congratulate all the girls, but the compliments sounded hollow. Several confided that the prettiest girl is always the runner-up. That was the wrong thing to say to me. I knew the prettiest girl had finished third and the most talented had won. There was all that comparing again. The fact was, I was just not quite up to par when it counted.

I had been Clebe McClary's little high-school girl friend. I had hoped that the Miss Florence crown would make me a somebody, that everyone would be after me, that Clebe would return to me or at least feel bad that he had dumped a beauty queen. Now I was really a nothing, a nobody.

It didn't help much a few days later when the paper carried a letter by a local merchant—Mr. Gladstone—bemoaning that the talent competition had seemed to dominate the contest. He insisted that he thought the whole picture should have been considered, and that Deanna Fowler had been the obvious winner. It was nice, I guess, but it didn't change anything.

I should have been thrilled when Valerie announced she was going to Europe to perform with an instrumental group and would not be able to carry out her Miss Florence duties. That afforded me many opportunities and advantages, but still I felt I was a pretender. I hadn't really won. I was just a fill-in, a substitute, an impostor.

I wallowed in self-pity, and no one knew how to pull me out of it, least of all me. I was able to get my mind on something else when Mother came home from the hospital and needed lots of attention and help. But as she grew stronger, she wanted to see me do the same.

"Deanna, honey, let's go down to the beach. You need to get out. We both do. You and Dean and Annette and Jennie and I will have a picnic down by the ocean, okay?"

We stayed at Ma-Ma Willis's house in Johnsonville, and Mother asked Ed Cribb, Clebe's best friend since high school, to spend a little time with me. She thought he could console me, give me some advice, get me on an even keel. He was manager of Oliver's Lodge Restaurant, and he had a better idea.

"Why don't y'all plan to eat at Oliver's tonight, and I'll see you there?"

I agreed to tag along for the day, secretly hoping we would run into Clebe, who was also working at Oliver's. Just in case, I wore my prettiest bathing suit, a white one with little boy legs and lace. While my brother and two little sisters cavorted in the water, I strolled down the beach, all the way to the other end from where Mother had set up our picnic. When I started back, I noticed a boy behind me.

At first I didn't think much of it, but each time I looked back, he seemed to be gaining on me. I tried to pick up my pace without being obvious. I looked back. He was hurrying, too. Now I was scared. I was too far from my family to call for help, and they couldn't see me. I didn't know whether I had anything to really be frightened of, but the dark stranger was getting closer.

Not hiding anything now, I lengthened my stride. I sneaked a peek back, and he had begun to run! I broke into a trot, and one more glance showed he was racing after me. I sprinted as hard and fast as I could, praying that the distance between us was enough that I could elude him until I reached Mother. I flew down that beach.

Mother looked up and smiled as I skidded to a stop. The boy had disappeared. I fought to regain my breath.

"A boy was chasing me, Mother."

She grew serious and headed back up the beach with me. She was fearless. If someone intended me harm, he would have to go through her first. We took a close look at some fishermen, and as we moved on, a boy approached.

"I can't believe the way you sped away from me, Deanna."

It was Jimmy, a boy I remembered from high school, a dreamboat everybody coveted, who had graduated two years before me. He was a clean-cut boy, very popular, a little shorter than Clebe, but a lot like him, too. I hadn't had the courage to even dream of dating him when he was in school, he was that special. And I had run from him! Was I embarrassed!

I apologized and told Jimmy I had been scared and hadn't waited around to see if my pursuer was friend or foe. We got acquainted and kidded each other for a while, and I realized that maybe I *could* be interested in someone other than Clebe. I was in Clebe's territory, and I wanted to see him and be seen by him; but here was a boy everyone wished to date—me included—and he was reminding me that I could have my head turned by someone else. Maybe, just maybe, I should start enjoying life again the way Clebe was.

That night at Oliver's Lodge, Ed treated us like royalty and introduced us to his friend, Ken Smith. He was a tall, good-looking guy who also reminded me of Clebe. He grabbed a chair, turned it backward, and sat right next to me, striking up a conversation.

Ed asked Mother if I could stay for a beach party and bonfire later. After dinner, he and Ken and my family walked out on the dock with me. While we were taking in the gorgeous sea and night sky, who should drive up in his Mustang but Clebe McClary. He was in fine form, perfectly cordial to everybody, not intimidated by running into the family of the girl whose heart he had broken. Clebe had lost none of his world-by-the-tail swagger. He seemed to have filled out, too, which made him look great, and I remember thinking that whoever he was dating was good for him.

"Hey there! How y'all doin'?"

My sister, Jennie, ten years old, stood gazing up at Ken, who stood next to me. I had no idea Ken and Clebe knew each other and had in fact agreed to room together at the University of South Carolina in the fall. After Clebe greeted Ken, Jennie piped up.

"What do you think of our new boy friend?"

I was mortified. As usual, Clebe was friendly and chivalrous.

"Hey! How 'bout that! Good to see y'all. I'm late pickin' up a date, so I gotta be goin'."

That comment dug so deeply into me that it is with me yet. I knew then that my relationship with Clebe was truly over. I told myself I might as well come to my senses, because I wasn't ever going to be Mrs. McClary. He had just finished me off.

Ed tried to tell me that night he'd like to see Clebe and me get back together, but I had lost hope. Ken paired off with me at the beach party and was a very sensitive, caring person. He rode with us when Ed took me back to my grandmother's house, and we laughed, kidded, traded stories, sang, and found ourselves comfortable with each other.

After Ken went home to Connecticut, we began corresponding, and Ed told me he thought Ken was getting serious about me. I couldn't believe it.

"After one date?"

The important thing was that I had begun to relax, to see that there were indeed other fish in the sea. I quit trying so hard to build and maintain relationships. I just enjoyed myself and others, appreciated their interest in me, and tried to see what qualities they possessed. How short-sighted I had been to think there was only one truly good person in the world! No one could measure up to Clebe, but not everyone else was a loser.

It wasn't long before Jimmy called and promised to never again chase me down the beach.

"But would you like to go out?"

I sure would! I grew to really like both him and Ken. I tried not to compare them with Clebe, but when I went to the beach with Jimmy, I secretly hoped Clebe would see us or at least hear about us. Down deep, though I hadn't admitted it even to myself yet, I wanted him back. I wasn't using my friendship with Jimmy to get to him, but I wouldn't have minded if the news of our relationship bothered Clebe.

It wasn't, however, my friendship with Jimmy that reached Clebe. It was Ken's interest in me.

CHAPTER 8

Surprise after Surprise

*T*hough I enjoyed developing a spontaneity more characteristic of me than when I had been with Clebe, I nursed a deep wound. And, I admit it, I still looked for a way—any way—to get back at Clebe.

At home I was miserable, rehashing the pain he had inflicted on me, vowing to never allow myself to be hurt like that again. My family commiserated with me, even Mother and Aunt Gee-Gee, the ones who had scolded me whenever I disagreed with Clebe or spoke up to him.

"He's too fine a young man and you are too lucky to have him to be risking it by treating him that way."

I had acquiesced, but look where it got me!

I tested my new style on Jimmy. I wanted him to accept me and my family for what we were. One night I greeted him with my face painted like Sadie Hawkins, a black tooth, bright red lips, a ponytail, the works. He turned on his heel as if heading back to the car without me. He laughed.

"I'm not takin' you anywhere lookin' like that!"

I said that was good because I didn't feel like going out. I just wanted to sit at home and visit with the family, maybe have some homemade dinner and play games. That was okay with Jimmy, and I liked that. I was being me. I wasn't hiding my family, and he was accepting them, too.

I thought that was pretty good. I could be ugly, and

Jimmy would still accept me. That was important. I had always thought that I had to be externally beautiful, fixed up perfectly for anybody to like me. Here I was, polka dots on my face, in essence wearing an ugly mask, trying to be true to myself, desperately trying to discover who I was.

I liked the new me, and I privately felt bolder about my response to Clebe, too.

I was mad, hurt, angry, vengeful, and I still cried at times. But I was not going to cave in, to grovel, to hide from the world. Though I enjoyed dating Jimmy a lot, I also looked forward to going to the University of South Carolina in the fall and dating Ken again. If that hurt Clebe, so much the better.

I didn't know Ed Cribb had already told Clebe that Ken was really interested in me. And I had no idea that Clebe had already called both my mother and my aunt, asking their forgiveness for the way he had treated me and the family, and asking their advice about trying to get back together with me. They advised him to lay low for a while and let them work on me. They weren't too subtle.

When I would pout and cry and threaten, rather than sympathize and add to their anti-Clebe reactions, they began to try to temper mine. That made me angrier. I felt I was developing strength, adding spontaneity to my life, being myself more. I thought it was healthy to quit worshiping Clebe and falling to my knees at his memory. It had been a mistake, I had become convinced, to pretend to be someone else around him. I had been wrong to let my family talk me out of speaking my mind when I dated him. I had become so weak and selfless that I had lost him. Maybe if I had been more independent and had a mind of my own, he would have respected me more. I wouldn't have seemed so young to him.

I didn't understand at all the change in attitude on the parts of my mother and aunt. I argued with them constantly about why they had all of a sudden forgiven him and started saying adoring things again, the way they had when he was around all the time. They justified it by saying that no one could be as bad as I was making him out to be. I took special comfort in the fact that Daddy was still on my side. I dare say he might have tried to hurt Clebe if he had showed up uninvited.

In spite of all those clues, I was still surprised when I heard from Clebe. I had built a protection zone around myself that I was determined would never, ever, allow me to be hurt like that again.

He wrote,

> I was wondering if you'd like to come down to your Aunt Gee-Gee's and we could go to the beach, maybe go out for some seafood, something like that. I have a graduation present for you that I never gave you.

I did *not* want to date him. I decided to tell him I had something else to do, but thanks for asking.

My mother was furious. So was Aunt Gee-Gee when she found out.

"What's the matter with you, girl? He's coming back to you, can't you see that? That's a fine boy, a fine young man. He's great. You're never gonna find anybody as nice as Clebe."

I couldn't believe it, and I told Mother so. "After all he's put me through, now my own loved ones are cramming him down my throat?"

Both Mother and Gee-Gee told me they were disappointed in me. "We can't believe the way you're acting, the turn you've taken after you loved that boy so long. You're being ridiculous. You need to get reacquainted with him. He's going to be a wonderful person."

"After what he did to me? Whose side are you on? I can't do anything right! The whole time I dated him you looked daggers at me every time I crossed him, so I suppressed my own opinions. You manipulated me because you were mature, experienced women. But no more. This is me, and I'm going to do what I think is right for once. I'm not going to listen to y'all. I don't want to be around him. I don't want to date him.

He's hurt me. If you think he's so wonderful, *you* date him."

I was angry, I was hurt, and no one could understand that I didn't need Clebe McClary forced on me. I wasn't ready for him just then. I hadn't had time to develop a plan for revenge, but the more I thought about how to answer him, the more I realized that a date with him at the beach might be a perfect opportunity. If he was, in fact, trying to win me back, I could wait until he got mushy and then react to him the way he had reacted to me the last time I had declared my love for him. I could hurt him, devastate him, humiliate him. I shudder to remember how vindictive I had become.

Occasionally, I caught myself wondering what he was doing. I knew he was working three jobs, including coaching the swimming team at Myrtle Beach, busing tables at Oliver's and working as a night clerk at The Breakers Hotel. Whenever I realized I was wondering about him, I forced myself to quit. I didn't want to be pining away over someone who had hurt me that deeply. I changed the subject in my mind by thinking about Jimmy or writing to Ken or dreaming about going to the university in the fall.

I confess that the one other aspect of his invitation that intrigued me was his mention of a gift. I always wished he had cared enough to give me a graduation gift. I couldn't erase from my mind the disappointment I'd felt when Clebe showed up with a gift wrapped in a ring box for me, only to find that the box held a pair of earrings from his mother.

Finally, I accepted his invitation for a date at the beach on July 26, 1966. Mother and I would stay with my aunt, and I would find out what this was all about. My plan was to let Clebe tell me he loved me, and then I would get even with him. I had allowed myself to fall head over heels in love with a man who suddenly lost interest and dumped me. I was not going to take it sitting down.

The closer I got to Aunt Gee-Gee's, the more specific and intricate my plan became. Not only was I going to do it, I was going to enjoy it. I was prepared to tell him that it was nice that he loved me, except that I was in love with somebody else now.

I didn't know with whom, but either Jimmy or Ken would certainly make an impact. Maybe I wouldn't name anyone, but just let him wonder.

Clebe and I went out to eat that night, and I was just waiting for him to get mushy. I was ready. He was as nice as ever to me—gentle, kind, considerate, caring—a real gentleman. We had a fun time, and he looked great. My plan was still intact, but he hadn't provided any openings.

We took a walk on the beach, and he held my hand. If a girl can communicate what she's really feeling and thinking by how she holds a guy's hand, I did that night. I was a limp rag, a dead fish. I wanted to yank my hand away and not even let him hold it, but I preferred making a statement. The fact that he wanted to hold my hand told me that he would eventually want to become romantic, and I rehearsed in my mind the many things I wanted to unload on him. Still, however, he was being sweet. I began to waver; my resolute plans were crumbling. It was hard to be mean or to even plan to be mean when he was making everything seem special.

It was a gorgeous moonlit night, and the phosphorus in the sand twinkled under the water like a million dazzling stars. I was like a hurt child, being distracted from her pain by a parent figure.

"Look at the phosphorus, Dea, like sparkling diamonds."

I was awe-struck. My plan was in deep jeopardy. I was nervous, wondering what was going to happen. Would I cave in on this first date after the long breakup? Could I maintain anger against this one who had been transformed almost overnight from the man of my dreams to the object of my revenge?

He talked and reminisced as we walked the beach. It was beautiful, but I couldn't even concentrate on everything he was saying. He was mostly trying to paint word pictures of what we saw. He also spoke of the mundane, the everyday, his three jobs, the swim team's record, that kind of stuff. As usual, he seemed to be overloading himself. My heart went out to him for the long hours he was putting in, but I wanted to get to the nitty-gritty. I wanted to hear an apology, a pleading for me to take him back, an explanation, an admission that he had come to his senses. Give me something, anything. An expression of love would have been shoved right back at him with venom. I was still prepared for that.

I wasn't prepared for a caper that took us onto the grounds of the old Huntington Castle where Clebe insisted that I climb wrought iron window bars to get to the poet's corner. I was baffled by his game.

"No! I don't want to go up there!"

"Be quiet! The night watchman might mistake us for prowlers and start shooting."

Great, that was all I needed.

"Clebe, I'm not climbing any more."

He reached for me with one hand, still clutching a large, flat present in the other.

"C'mon, Dea, it's not that much farther. I have to give you your graduation present in a special place. It'll mean that much more to you."

By the time we got up there, the mosquitoes were horrible. I slapped several dozen away every few seconds, but the ones that avoided my attacks left huge welts and started me complaining.

"Clebe, come on, let's get down from here! These mosquitoes are about to kill me. They're swarming all over me. We're gonna get malaria if we don't get out of here."

"Just a minute, honey, I want to give you your present."

It wasn't until later that I realized he had called me something other than Deanna or Dea. I just wanted to get this over with.

"Let's please hurry, Clebe. I want to get out of this scary place and away from these giant mosquitoes."

He handed me the present, which I tore open quickly. In the darkness I could tell it was a book, but I couldn't see what it was. I was impatient.

"What is this, Clebe?"

"It's a book on all the plantations we've toured, Dea."

What I said next was not what I meant. "Oh, Clebe, it's beautiful. Thank you so much. Now can we go?"

He was ignoring me. He stood there talking in a low, soothing tone, and I didn't know whether he was just trying to work up the courage to kiss me or what. I hugged him quickly and pleaded with him to take me out of there. I wanted to tell him that I found it hard to believe I had endured a risky, ridiculous climb to the roof of a castle to receive some dumb book. But now that I had it, let's go.

I held the book in my right hand and used it to swat at the ever-attacking pests. Clebe spoke nervously as he idly played with my birthstone ring, twisting and twisting it as he spoke.

"Clebe, please!"

He just kept talking.

I hunched my shoulders, trying to kill bugs on my cheek. "Clebe, I'm serious. I hate these things. They're driving me crazy. Aren't they biting you? I can't stand it. Let's go out of here now!" I swatted and scratched and wiggled, trying to pull away from him.

He kept talking. "Yeah, they are kind of bad tonight. So, honey, what's your answer?"

"My answer?"

"Yeah. What's your answer?"

"To what?"

"I'm not going to ask you again. Just look at your hand."

I looked at the hand holding the book, wondering if it had swollen from a nasty bite. Clebe grabbed my left wrist and raised it to the moonlight. My birthstone ring was aflame. But no. It wasn't my birthstone ring. It was a new ring. A diamond.

My plan flew out the window. I didn't know what in the world to do. I was in shock.

"Clebe, let's get down now."

When we finally reached the ground and headed back to the beach, Clebe put his arm around me.

"So, what's your answer?"

"Would you mind telling me what you asked me up there?"

"Well, I think I asked you to marry me."

Talk about catching somebody off guard! I had been worried that he might want to get romantic, and now this! All I could think of was that I had to marry him. Not because I wanted to. Not because I loved him. Not because he was the only person in the world to me. Not because we were back together or because it was the right thing. It was almost as if I felt obligated.

He had put a ring on my finger, and I couldn't disappoint him. He had crushed me, but I couldn't reciprocate. I had planned to turn the tables on him, but I knew he had been rejected before, and since he had rejected me, I knew how that felt. I couldn't let him endure that again. Not two broken engagements for the same wonderful man.

I wasn't excited. I didn't want to be engaged. I wasn't sure I wanted to get married that young either. But I couldn't hurt him. I was confused, unsure of what to do or say.

"Oh, yes, yes. I'd love to marry you."

I threw my arms around him, and we kissed. I tried to act real excited, and I agreed that we should run and tell Ed at Oliver's. I didn't feel sincere. I was scared to death, horrified. It was so quick. All I could think of was not hurting his feelings. I figured I had to be married now, no matter what. The ring was a seal, so I supposed the marriage would have to happen.

I acted happy because I wanted Clebe to be happy, but through the entire evening, I felt out of control. I went through the motions of showing people and acting thrilled, all the while asking myself why things like this always seemed to happen to me. When I thought of the number of times I had wished and hoped and prayed that Clebe would propose, and now here was a time when it was the last thing I wanted, and guess what? He pops the question.

We showed the ring to his parents that night. His mother

kidded about looking at the diamond through a magnifying glass.

The next morning we invited Mother and Gee-Gee to meet us down at the beach. When we spotted them, we ran to them.

"We're engaged! We're engaged! Look! We're engaged!"

Though Mother and Gee-Gee had encouraged this renewal of our relationship, they didn't believe this new twist. Gee-Gee took my finger in hers and studied the stone in the sunlight. Remembering the trick I'd played on them before, she asked, "What drugstore did you buy this from?"

We all laughed, but I saw Mother's and Gee-Gee's smiles fade when they realized we were dead serious. Mother spoke up, right in front of Clebe and Gee-Gee.

"Deanna, are you sure? Is this something you really want to do? This is a big step, a major decision. This is your life. You realize that just the other day you were telling me you never wanted to see Clebe again as long as you lived. He'd hurt you. He'd broken your heart. Now all of a sudden, here you are, flitting all around and acting happy as a lark. Now you want to marry him?"

I thought that was what she wanted and that she would be thrilled. Now that a ring was on my finger, things were more serious than she had anticipated and she'd gone through a personality change. I had been running on autopilot, not thinking, not having time to reflect. I spoke softly, directly to Clebe, but Mother and Gee-Gee could hear.

"Clebe, you know Mother's right. Here I've been so upset with you, and this is not at all part of what I had planned. I'm terribly confused. I don't know what I should do. I don't want to hurt your feelings."

"What do you mean, you don't know what you should do? I asked you to marry me, and you said yes. What you should do is marry me."

"But, Clebe, this is all so sudden. I'm scared. I'm so confused. Clebe, just keep the ring, and one day maybe it will work out for us. This is all too much for me right now."

I held the ring out to him, but he made no move to take it. I could see from his face that I had administered the cruelest, most humiliating revenge, even though I had given up on that plan. Nothing I had planned to say was as bad as what I had just said. His color was gone; his eyes were glazed. He stared right through me. When he spoke, his voice was choked with emotion. He was angry and hurt.

"I'm not takin' another ring back. You keep it. If you ever decide you want to marry me, you just put that ring on and let me know. I've always wanted to go to Australia, so that's where I'm goin'."

He hung his head, and my heart ached for him. His pain was magnified in me.

CHAPTER 9

The Best,
The Proud,
The Few

*C*lebe had often talked about wanting to go to Australia to train for track competition in the Olympics, but it had been just a dream. I didn't think he'd leave for Australia now that his graduate school and coaching plans were in place, but who could know?

What I did know was that I had hurt Clebe deeply. He had hurt me, too, of course, but even in my darkest plots of how to get back at him, I never intended this. To accept a marriage proposal—which was a foolish thing to do in the state I was in—and then renege on it the next day was as low a blow as any person should have to take.

My goal was to think about what I had done and try to heal the wound I had inflicted on Clebe, but I didn't want to change my mind again just so he would feel better. That would have been disastrous. I didn't want to fake excitement again and have him think I was as thrilled as he was at our marriage prospects. Ours had been such a frustrating and confusing relationship, I could hardly believe where we'd been.

I had bought that fake diamond when we had dated only several months. That had scared *him*. Then he'd wanted to go steady after we'd dated just a few months, and *I* wasn't ready, even though I loved him with all my heart and dreamed of marrying him. Not long after that, I wore his ring and we went steady, but I *did* let someone else take me to the prom. I hadn't really wanted to date anyone else, but *Clebe* didn't like it. It may have had something to do with his deciding that we both needed our freedom, especially me. *I* didn't want that and accepted it only as something to be mourned as deeply as a divorce.

I finally got out and started enjoying life again, all the while still pining for Clebe, longing either to have him back or to hurt him the way he had hurt me. Suddenly *he'd* swung all the way over to where I had been. He wanted to be married. I agreed, so as not to hurt his feelings, then realized through Mother's warnings (a change of heart on her part, too!) that I had been hasty, and pulled the rug out from under him.

So there I was, finally maturing, finally deciding to stop this pendulum of emotions. Maybe I owed Clebe an apology. Maybe I owed it to him to give his ring back against his protests and tell him—the way he had told me before—that this was really for the best and we would do each other a favor by waiting a while. I didn't know. I simply didn't want to react impulsively again, the way each of us had so many times.

I quit writing Ken and dating Jimmy, and I thought about Clebe every waking moment. I was angry with my mother and and my aunt for forcing me to see him again. If I had stuck to my guns and refused to see him for a while, I wouldn't have been in this mess. I knew he was hurt, and I even knew he probably deserved to be for the way he had treated me and my love, but something made me feel for him in his pain.

After several days of brooding, thinking, praying, talking to my mother, and trying to plan for college in the fall, one fact couldn't be pushed from my heart and mind. There was one reason I could feel sorry for Clebe after I had merely treated him the way he had treated me. That could mean only one thing: I loved him. I truly loved him. He had his faults; it was good I finally saw that. I had developed some independence, the ability to think for myself and express myself. That was good, too. But it didn't change the fact that I loved Clebe Mc-Clary.

All those qualities that drew people to him, that charmed

everyone with whom he came in contact, his gentleness, his can-do attitude, his healthy competitive spirit, his knowledge of nature, they were all still intact. In spite of the mistakes he had made and his insensitivity to me, he was still a wonderful, charming, complete man, respected, admired, and godly.

He wrote me sweet letters during that time. He didn't push. He simply expressed his love to me. He talked of being at the University of South Carolina with me in the fall. He asked about my family. That was another major factor. I never realized, until I had "lost" Clebe, how special he was to my family. I knew they got along and liked one another, but I had no idea the depth of the affection between him and my brother and sisters. For Dean, Jr., Clebe was the brother he never had. Annette once wrote me that she hoped to one day marry someone half as great as Clebe. Little Jennie was madly, unabashedly, in love with him the first time she met him.

Through occasional comments and some overt cheerleading on my mother's part, I began to see that I would not disappoint my family if I welcomed Clebe back into my life. Daddy, however, was a different story. He hadn't been told about the marriage proposal. In fact, he wasn't aware I had even seen Clebe again. That beautiful diamond I occasionally pulled from its little box under my mattress was Mother's and my secret. When Daddy wasn't around, I put it on and dreamed of walking the aisle to meet Clebe at the altar.

The whole time I would ask myself, "Is this right? Is it what I need?" And I would pray, "Lord, please don't let me make a mistake."

It wasn't long before I realized that my heart was racing ahead of me. I had tried to keep everything at a logical level, to reason it out, decide whether I was still vengeful, whether acquiescing to Clebe's proposal would be just a kind gesture or the right thing for the rest of my life.

But the thinking had been done. The heart had taken over. My letters to Clebe became warmer, more affectionate, more loving without being overt. I didn't want to falsely encourage him. He wrote no more about Australia, so I knew that had been simply a threat in the heat of disappointment. But something was happening to me. I was in love with Clebe. I had never lost that love; it had simply been hidden by disappointment, grief, vengeance, bitterness, mourning.

Finally I was ready to tell somebody.

"Mother, I know I love Clebe. I really do love him. I feel secure and happy when I think about him, and I believe we'd make a perfect couple. My problem was that y'all harped on me so much that I didn't even want to date him anymore. But I'm past that now. I've thought it through, and I want him back."

Mama did not smile. She was happy, but she was also aware how serious this situation was. Her eldest daughter was making the biggest decision of her life.

"Have you made the decision, honey?"

"Yes."

"You're accepting his proposal?"

"Yes. Don't you think it will be all right, Mother?"

"It's your decision, and you're going to have to live with it."

"I know."

"I don't know what your daddy's gonna think."

"Let's worry about that later, Mother. I want to tell Clebe we're engaged. Then we'll let Clebe talk to Daddy."

Mother drove me to Myrtle Beach where Clebe was coaching the swim team. I was so excited I thought my heart would burst. I wouldn't demand explanations. I wouldn't require apologies. I didn't have an agenda of agreements that set the past in order. All I wanted was to show Clebe I was wearing the diamond ring he had bought me. That would say it all. We would go back to being simply in love. Not just friends. We would be committed to each other now and forever, the way I had always wanted it.

When we pulled up, it began to rain.

Oh no! Here I'm about to tell my fiancé that we're engaged, and my hair is going to look a mess!

Clebe had his back to us, intensely working with the diving team. I decided the rain and my hair were least important. I opened the door and waved to him with my left hand, hoping he'd see the diamond, though the clouds had covered the sun.

"Clebe! Clebe!"

The rain fell harder. He stood and turned around, searching for the source of the voice. I ran toward him, calling his name. He broke into a run, too, a huge smile creasing his face. I wrapped my arms around him and kissed him, then held up my ringed hand. He lifted me and swung me around as he kissed me again.

"We're engaged. Clebe, I love you."

He let out a holler that brought his swimmers and divers scrambling out of the pool. Clebe set me down and ran toward his team. He looked back at me.

"C'mon, darlin'! Quick!"

I followed him.

"Hey, ever'body, I want to introduce you to my fiancée! We're goin' to be married!"

The rain fell in sheets as the wet bodies gathered around, jumping all over me, hugging and kissing me. Clebe fought through them to embrace me one more time with his team cheering him on. We kissed, then ran for shelter. It was clear Clebe was as happy as I was. Despite all we had been through, that day couldn't have been better. We would never look back, never borrow yesterday's problems. We would face enough new ones over the years, but that day we buried the bad memories and solidified the good ones.

Fortunately, Daddy took the news better than I had any reason to expect. He'd always been a fan of Clebe's. But when Clebe broke up with me and Daddy got only my side of the story, he was ready to kill him if that had been what I wanted. Now, with a little explaining, Daddy was just as ready and willing to accept Clebe into the family. If that was what his daughter wanted, that's how it would be. If Clebe was okay with Deanna, he was okay with Daddy.

"Just remember, son, sticks, stacks, no take back!"

* * *

There wasn't much time before we all had to head to the University of South Carolina. Clebe felt strongly that I should finish college, and we even discussed waiting to get married until then. He would finish his master's in a couple of years and be coaching under Paul Dietzel, and when we were both out of school, we would marry.

I was willing to marry him right then or wait ten years, whatever he wanted. As long as I knew I was his and he was mine, I was happy to know we would one day be married. I was still eighteen, and though I felt no pressure or problem with already being committed to someone for a lifetime at such a young age, I wasn't dying to get married right away.

Until . . .

Clebe moved his belongings into an apartment with Ken Smith a couple of weeks before classes were to start. Almost immediately, Clebe realized he didn't fit in with the campus scene. Almost all the students at the university, especially the younger ones, were growing their hair long and dressing sloppily to show their rebellion against and dissatisfaction with the Vietnam War.

Clebe was a patriot, born and bred. He'd always felt he should be an example, not blindly following his government, but loyally standing with America in its defense of freedom and its effort to halt the spread of tyranny and communism. As a coach, he had worn his hair short and insisted—against the protestations of many students and parents—that his athletes do the same. He was convinced that the length of a man's hair was a statement and that you could tell his politics and his character from it. If a man always rebelled and protested, he was likely to be an unkempt hippie type. There were exceptions, of course, and Clebe even admits that there were problems with the Vietnam War and the government's policies in it. But he never believed, and doesn't to this day, that anything was accomplished by a bunch of kids letting their hair grow long, staging sit-ins, love-ins, and sleep-ins, doing drugs, and carrying banners that made them look like traitors.

When college buildings across America were shut down or bombed or burned, Clebe was sickened. He didn't want to be counted with those who went into coaching or stayed in school to evade the draft. He felt, as an older student, that he had a moral obligation to be an example. When a friend casually asked him if he had served his country in the armed forces, Clebe was embarrassed to say that he hadn't. He soon came to me with the news of a decision that established clearly the differences between a mature, grown man and a young, recent high-school graduate. It was a decision that changed our immediate plans, our long-range plans, and ultimately our entire lives. It was a decision that would shape us and our family forever, but we certainly didn't know that at the time.

"Dea, I need to serve my country. This is a time for action, and I want to enlist."

"Enlist. Enlist in what?"

"I've always wanted to be a Marine."

"You want to go into the military?"

He nodded.

I panicked. "Clebe! Everything is set. We're engaged. I'm on my way to school. You're getting settled in. It's all so perfect. The war won't be affected by whether you're involved. Don't do this."

Over the next several days, Clebe wrestled with his decision, and I wrestled with him. I was tenacious. As firmly as he believed he had to do this, I believed it was the worst idea he could have. Of course, he was thinking of his country. I was thinking of us. I lobbied hard and long against it. I begged; I pleaded; I cried. I planned ways he could serve without really enlisting. I recruited friends to try to talk him out of it. But the same stubbornness and iron will I so admired in him made him hold firmly to his decision. He was impossible to argue with, though I tried everything. Once he made up his mind, it was as good as done.

I argued that the reason I had enrolled at Carolina was to be with him. He reminded me that I had not changed my plans when we had split up.

"But, Clebe, now that we're engaged and committed to each other, I don't want to be there while you're somewhere else."

My daddy was no help. As a former Marine navigator in World War II (he often reminded us that there was no such thing as an ex-Marine), he quickly warmed to the idea. "If you're gonna be in the military, Clebe, then you join the best, the proud, the few: the Marine Corps."

Clebe told me he had wanted to join the Marines right out of high school, but his father wouldn't allow it. Now his father and my father were proud of his choice. I was frantic. I told Clebe it wasn't fair that a twenty-six-year-old man, just two months from the end of his draft eligibility, should even have to consider joining the military.

"Everybody else is getting deferments for college, divinity school, hangnails, Sunday school, you name it. Why can't you find a way to evade the draft? Stay in school. Why do *you* have to be the one who serves?"

"Deanna."

That was all he had to say. No one can silence me for long, but when Clebe is finished arguing, or when I have put forth a totally transparent, selfish viewpoint, he has a way of shutting it down. I had to take a different tack. It may have been just strategy at first, but as soon as it was out of my mouth, I embraced the idea.

"Well, if you're going to be in the military, so am I."

"Deanna, that's ridiculous."

"No, it isn't. I want to go wherever you go. Let's go ahead and get married now, and we'll go together."

"No, now, Deanna, this is serious. This is no game."

"I'm not playing a game, honey. I know it's serious. If this is what you're going to do, it puts a different light on our plans. We should be married first. That will affect where you go, where you're housed, where you're stationed, and everything, won't it?"

"Whoa, slow down, Dea. Yes, it puts a different light on our plans. If I go into the military, we'll wait till I get out to get married. You'll be through with school by then, so it's the same amount of time. The difference is that we will not be together much during those four years."

"You make that sound so insignificant. I don't want you in the military if it means we won't be together. I was looking forward to being out on my own at college, but not without you!"

He spoke with finality, even though I knew he hadn't made up his mind and he, too, was agonizing over the decision.

"Our marriage is goin' to have to wait until I fulfill my military obligation. I definitely don't want to get married right now and have both those responsibilities on me."

All I could think of was, *Here we go again. Things always changed in our relationship. We thought it was set, but it's not.* I was confident that my next several years were settled. I had my life's partner, I was starting four years of college, and now here he comes with more decisions. I'll never forget the night everyone sat around talking about Clebe's decision for hours at our family beach house, trying to help him sort through the facts and make sure he was making the right decision. Up until then I really thought I could dissuade him, but by the end of the evening, I knew it was decided. The best I could hope for was that he would agree that we should be married first. Of course, I also hoped that his vision would be bad or that his flat feet would look even flatter at his induction physical, but that was absurd.

Clebe passed the physical with flying colors. I had been looking for ways out. He had been looking for ways in, reasons to serve. I wasn't thinking about our country or our freedom. I wasn't patriotic. I was selfish. I now have a great sense of pride that my husband made all but the ultimate sacrifice in the service of his country, and it nearly moves me to tears when strangers approach Clebe and merely thank him for giving his eye and his arm for their freedom.

Because I had been obsessed with my, me, mine, it took a long time to adjust to the total reverse of momentum when

Clebe decided to follow through with his plan. Instead of being away from my family in Columbia with the man I loved, I would be alone in the big city with no security. I had planned the best of both worlds: getting out on my own and leaving my secure, though sometimes turbulent, home, yet having Clebe within walking distance. Now my plans were ruined.

I had planned to study psychology for the same reason most students do: to learn about myself. I wasn't in class two weeks before I realized I could just as easily lose myself as find myself in psychology. I was not adventurous and independent. Being out on my own was not as great as I thought. Clebe had been assigned to Parris Island, and I simply did not want to be at USC without him.

I transferred to Francis Marion back in Florence; if I couldn't be with Clebe, I could at least live at home. I also switched majors. As soon as I made the change, I knew it was what I had wanted all along. I was going into nursing. While Clebe took off to boot camp, I took to nursing like I was born to it.

Now if I could just talk Clebe into getting married before he got too far along in his military career and got assigned somewhere without me . . .

10

Marital Boot Camp

*I*plunged into nurse's training while Clebe suffered through boot camp, then Officer Candidate School (OCS) at Quantico, Virginia. He would come out of there a second lieutenant and then attend twenty-one weeks in the Basic School for advanced training. At some point during this time he became convinced that we should be married between those two schools. Clebe believed that after he became commissioned, he could support a wife and have a future to offer me. We weren't sure exactly when that would be, but the Marine Corps narrowed it to sometime around April Fools' Day, which became a standing joke with us.

If we could work in the wedding before the Basic School, we could live in officers' housing in Quantico before Clebe was assigned permanent orders. I couldn't believe my good fortune. One thing I pushed from my mind: Marine second lieutenants were being shipped directly to action in Vietnam as quickly as they could be trained and processed. Maybe if I didn't allow myself to think about it, it wouldn't happen.

I learned enough about the war to know I didn't want Clebe in Vietnam. Because they had to lead battalions into any skirmish, second lieutenants were the first to die in combat, and I knew Clebe liked to be where the action was. I had even heard him talk about reconnaissance duty during the Basic School. He wouldn't be specific with me about it, so I asked one of his friends what it was all about. I learned that recon teams lead the way and scout areas behind enemy lines in advance of the rest of the troops. It sounded like a suicide mission to me. I made Clebe promise me he would not volunteer or even allow himself to be chosen for recon duty, though we both knew it sounded like just what he would enjoy.

I loved nursing school and made friends quickly. I was nominated for several class positions, but as a letter to Clebe from that period makes clear, I was planning yet another move. I would drop out for a semester or two to get married, then take up my studies again somewhere else if Clebe was sent overseas. He had expressed his fears to me that it would be difficult for a young woman, newly married, to remain faithful while her husband was away. I tried to allay his fears in my letter:

> You know yourself that I would be much better married those six months before you go overseas. Darling, all I can do is pray that you will trust me and have faith in me. How do you think it would make me feel to know that my husband couldn't trust me while he was away? If you have any doubts of my love for you, and if you don't think that I'll be true to you when we're apart, then we shouldn't get married. Because, darling, with you coaching one day and me nursing, there will be times when we'll be apart. . . .
>
> Darling, I can't begin to tell you how happy you have made me. I don't care if it *is* April Fools' Day when we get married. Just so you don't pop up at the church and say, "April Fool!" The nurses have already planned a shower for me. They said they couldn't wait.
>
> More people remark about what a good couple we make. They say we look like we were always meant to be together. As for the school nominations, I'll turn them all down. I'd rather have a husband like you than anything else I could ever be awarded. . . .

I love you so much, Lt. McClary. Hope you won't mind when we're married if I kiss you good-bye every day instead of saluting. I love you.

It's a wonder I could keep my attention on my studies and my student nursing with marriage on my mind. One of my first patients was a big, heavy man who'd had a heart attack and then heart surgery. For an early exam I was to change his bed with him in it. This was long before the now widely accepted practice of getting heart surgery patients up and walking as soon as possible.

I was so nervous about the exam, with the irrepressible instructor, Mrs. Rice, coming to personally check my work, that I did a horrible job. The man was so sweet. He kept asking what he could do to help. I rolled him one way and loosened the sheets on that side. Then I rolled him the other way and loosened them on that side. By making him roll back and forth, I was able to get half the bed made, but it was a mess. The man was so large I didn't have much bed to work with, and I panicked.

"Do you really want to help, sir?"

"Anything, darlin'."

"If I helped you, do you think you could get to that chair? I can make this bed in no time and get you right back into it."

"Let's do it."

He was in the chair, looking pale and breathing heavily, and I was quickly making the bed when Miss Rice walked in. She glared and scowled and quietly helped me finish and get him back into bed. In the hall, I got both barrels.

"Wouldn't you say, Miss Fowler, that risking a man's life for your grade is a bit extreme? That was ridiculous. You have better sense than that."

Better sense and a worse grade. When I thought about it, I was as shaken as she was about what could have happened.

Finally, we got official word from the Marine Corps. Clebe would be commissioned a second lieutenant on Good

Friday, March 24, 1967. He would then have the weekend and a few days of leave. We set the date for our wedding, Easter Day, March 26.

Clebe's commanding officer tried to dissuade him from getting married, telling Clebe he would be out in the bush for six months following the wedding. Clebe told me I would see him only two days a week during that time, even if I lived in officers' quarters on the base. While making him a second lieutenant, the Corps would also prepare him for Vietnam. I wrote immediately to put Clebe's mind at ease:

> I'm glad your commanding officer [finally] understands our plans. So many officers might have forgotten what it was like to be separated from the one you love. Of course I will be happy to even spend two days a week with you. Anything is better than not at all. We can enjoy each other for those two days anyway. I certainly understand, so don't worry. We'll just combine a week into two days. . . .

In that same letter I was darkly prophetic without knowing it. Today these words leap out at me, and I wonder if God planted a premonition to prepare both of us for what lay ahead:

> There will probably be many things, but we'll meet life's problems together. Nothing or no one could break the tie that binds our love as one.
>
> I love you, darling, and want only for you to love me. I'm eagerly looking forward to Easter. I will certainly have forgotten how to kiss by then, but as I recall, it was sure a lot of fun learning. Just think, we'll be celebrating our anniversary on such a wonderful day.

I was nervous about my honeymoon night and what it was supposed to be like. I had a vague idea about what I was to do

Mrs. Patrick Cleburn McClary III, committed to love at the age of nineteen.

Mother, Daddy, and me. Though Daddy said he named me, Carol Deanna, after the singer Deanna Durbin, I knew he named me after Mother and himself—Caroline and Dean.

Annette, me, and Dean (left to right). My role as the first-born made me feel like the protector of the other children.

Dean and me at Goggie's boarding house. I'm wearing the hula skirt from Miss Jane Hemingway.

Goggie and Paw Paw at their fiftieth wedding anniversary.

Keynotes, the chorus of Moore Junior High School. I loved to sing, and in junior high school, Miss Betty Ann Darby selected me to be in the chorus that traveled around the state.

1965 CHEERLEADERS

Left to right: Deanna Fowler, Karen McElveen, alternate, Brenda Creel, Robert Herring, Anne Malone, Claudia Young, Sharon Ellis.

Absent when picture was made: Linda Lawrence, alternate, Peggy Hutchinson, Dayle Marchette.

Cheerleading days at McClenaghan High School.

I was first runner-up in the Miss Florence Contest. Valerie Bobbitt (winner), Sue Smith, and Judy Way (left to right). I had believed that if I could win the contest, I would be worthy of Clebe's love.

Clebe's graduation photo from Erskine College.

Clebe when I first started dating him. He was an athletic man's man who seemed too good to be true.

Clebe's graduation day from Officer Candidate School at Quantico, Virginia.

Clebe's and my wedding day. Clebe was the most handsome Marine,
the best husband a girl could have.

Clebe in Vietnam. I lived in terror, day to day, waiting for news of Clebe's death. But he wrote faithfully to reassure us of his condition.

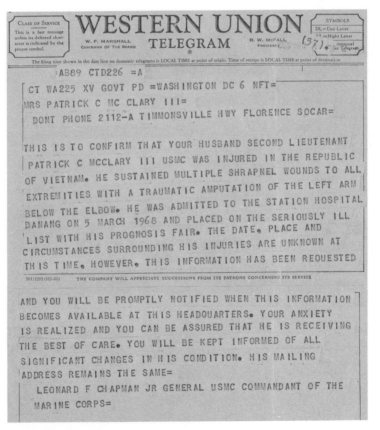

The second of the many telegrams I would receive reporting Clebe's injury in Quang Nam.

Meeting General Chapman at Bethesda Naval Hospital.

Clebe, me, and Senator Strom Thurmond. Senator Thurmond was instrumental in having Clebe flown from Vietnam to Bethesda Naval Hospital.

Clebe on leave from Philadelphia Naval Hospital. Clebe looked like misery personified. But he never lost his determination, his inner strength and integrity.

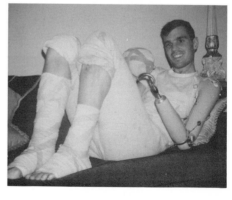

Clebe on his first leave from Philadelphia Naval Hospital
to coach.

Billy Zeoli and me. Billy's crusade message at my
high-school football stadium turned both Clebe and
me to the Lord.

Clebe and Pa Pa at Anaheim Stadium before speaking at the Billy Graham Crusade. Clebe's commitment to Christ opened the door for him to speak at crusades around the country.

Clebe's office at the Way, the coffee house youth center we opened in the basement of the old post office building in Georgetown.

Tara, Clebe, me, and Christa at a crusade. We are committed to each other as a family and committed to serve the Lord together.

Christa Annette McClary, 17 years old. Christa and Clebe are
look alikes.

Tara Deanna McClary, 19 years old. Tara and I are look alikes.

Dove Eludes McClary

1983

Staff and AP Reports

A Florence native, Deanna McClary, lost in her bid for a Dove Award this week.

The awards were presented Wednesday night in Nashville, Tenn. They go each year to the top gospel recording artists in America.

Mrs. McClary, who now lives in Pawleys Island, had been nominated in two categories, both Female Vocalist of the Year and Gospel Artist of the Year.

Amy Grant, who won a Grammy award for her hit album "Age to Age," followed with two Dove awards Wednesday night and was named Gospel Artist of the Year.

Miss Grant, 22, was presented Contemporary Gospel Album of the Year and Album Cover of the Year for "Age to Age" at the Gospel Music Association's 14th annual Dove Awards Show.

Sandi Patti, who was last year's Female Vocalist of the Year, repeated in that category this year and also won an award for Inspirational Gospel Album for her "Lift Up the Lord."

Mrs. McClary, daughter of Mr. and Mrs. Dean Fowler of Florence, and the other nominees received a compliment from Miss Grant after her win.

"Everybody in my category is a winner," the Nashville native said backstage at the Tennessee Performing Arts Center. "We all express ourselves so differently."

Her album, with 250,000 copies sold, is one of the biggest selling gospel albums ever and was No. 1 on the gospel charts for more than six months.

Larnelle Harris won Doves for Male Vocalist of the Year and Black Inspirational Gospel Album for "Touch Me Lord."

Al Green's "Precious Lord," which won a Grammy in February, won a Dove for Black Traditional Gospel Album.

The Imperials won a Dove for the Group of the Year, while Michael Card and Jon Thompson won Song of the Year for "El Shaddai."

Country singer Barbara Mandrell's album "He Set My Life To Music" won in the category Gospel Album of the Year By a Secular Artist.

Deanna McClary: a 'Proud Moment'

Deanna McClary did not receive the Dove Award this year (as was reported in the *Morning News*), but can you imagine how proud her family and friends are that she was in the top five finalists for Gospel Artist of the Year?

Perhaps it would have been more appropriate if the article reporting her achievement had been introduced in big, bold print as follows: "Florence Is Proud of Deanna McClary, One of Top Five Gospel Artists of 1982."

When the winner, Amy Grant, was interviewed, she said it so well, "All of the nominees are winners. Each one has a different method of expression."

I was in Nashville April 13, along with Deanna's husband, Clebe, and daughters, Tara and Christa. When Deanna's name was called out as one of the nominees for Gospel Artist of the Year, we were proud of her and thanked God for his blessing of bringing her to that moment. It was truly a great moment for us, and for the City of Florence.

My album cover for *Deanna*. As I became a known singer, I recorded several albums and was even nominated for two Dove awards. But my primary ministry has always been and always will be to be Clebe's wife, Mrs. Clebe McClary.

Ralph Carmichael and me at the 1983 Dove awards.

Talking with a Vietnam vet. My commitment to Clebe amidst his pain and rehabilitation has given me a deep love for and commitment to other Vietnam veterans.

Christa; Jennie's son, Edward; Deanna's sister, Jennie; and Tara.

Clebe, me, Tara, and Christa. Tara and Christa are the fruit of Clebe's and my commitment to love each other.

Starting the long hike up Pike's Peak. My husband has always pushed himself to the limit. And I'm not about to let him go by himself.

Clebe and I have decided to remarry for our twenty-fifth anniversary. Because of all that we've been through together, we've truly become a team. And now more than ever, I'm committed to love my husband.

and how I was to respond, but then my physician, Dr. Albert Baroody, told me not to "take the sex manual" with me. He said to do what came naturally, be loving, and be relaxed. If we were considerate of each other, he assured me, we should have no problem.

Of course my mother tried to explain to me what I should expect, and we were both grateful that I was inexperienced and had no one and nothing to compare Clebe or my first sexual experience to. She told me never to become a wife who deprives her husband, especially of something as important as physical love. "Take care of your man" was the idea.

I wrote Clebe,

Yes, I have been reading about marriage and so forth, but I will leave the teaching up to you. Of course, we will both be learning a great deal from each other. I'm really looking forward to being even closer than ever to my sweetheart, and my body will become yours. Just having my darling near me with your arms around me has been so very wonderful.

Many things have happened since that Wednesday night at the mall in October of 1965, some wonderful and some not so wonderful. But the fact that my life will continue to revolve around yours makes everything perfect. I want so much to make you the happiest boy in the world. All I ask in return is you and your love.

I love it when you tell me that there are many boys that are richer and better looking than you but that I will never find one that loves me more than you do and who wants to give me a good home, not just a house, but a home. What boy would say something like that? No one but the most precious person in my life: you.

Money, a beautiful home, and luxury are things lots of girls search for in the man they marry. But I will be a queen when I marry someone as rich in words and deeds as you. I am so proud of you, Clebe, and I'm sure OCS is proud of having an outstanding candidate like you.

As our wedding plans shifted into high gear, many friends in Florence and Georgetown hosted beautiful showers and parties for me. It was sad that Clebe was unable to leave Quantico for any of them, but even worse, I was unable to attend his graduation and commissioning because I was so busy with wedding preparations. I'm glad his sister, Patty, was able to attend and pin his bars on his uniform. The next day they drove to Florence for the rehearsal party at Goggie's home.

The stage was set for a storybook wedding. The rehearsal went smoothly the night before—we used stand-ins for the bride and groom—and Easter Day dawned in full bloom. Cherokee Road was emblazoned with color, dogwoods flaming pink and white, azaleas beautiful and fragrant, the sky cloudless and bright.

For some reason, I was almost late to my own wedding. I was chronically late anyway, so there were those who wondered if I'd make it. I don't remember if I forgot something or Daddy did, but for whatever reason, we were halfway to the church and had to go back home, so it was a whirlwind trip. Suffice it to say, Daddy sped both ways.

After hurrying to dress with the aid of my bridesmaids, I heard the lovely organ music emanating from the sanctuary. Several soloists performed, but I was most touched by Jennie, then twelve, who sang so beautifully that she moved several to tears. Many people said she sang "Whither Thou Goest" like an angel. I was so proud of her.

My heart pounded as each of the girls kissed me before making their way down the aisle. When the organ resounded with the processional, I felt like a princess meeting her prince. In keeping with tradition, I hadn't seen Clebe all day. Now, at four in the afternoon, I stood in the back, gazing up the aisle at the spot where my beloved would stand. As he came into view in his beautiful dress blue uniform (the first time I'd ever seen it) and stood at parade rest with his hands behind him, I burst with pride. He looked more debonair than ever, and he glowed.

Mr. Pat, Clebe's dad, was best man and stood next to his son, ramrod straight. He looked so happy for both of us! I appreciated him and was eager to see our families joined.

As my father, so handsome and tall and strong, stood next to me and quietly exulted over "that handsome Marine" waiting for me, I felt a deep sense of joy and satisfaction that I had saved myself for Clebe. I was wearing the white dress and veil with pride and sincerity. It represented the purity I offered Clebe as a wedding present.

Daddy was nervous about giving away his first daughter, and when I hugged him, I saw tears in his eyes. The walk down the aisle, with Clebe's and my best friends waiting on either side, would be the last walk Daddy and I would take as Fowlers. I would soon become a McClary, and though I couldn't have been happier, that was a melancholy moment.

We had snafus typical of weddings. I had cut the base of my left glove at the ring finger so I could just slip that off and Clebe could put the ring on. I forgot to tell him, so during the prayer, just before the exchange of rings, Clebe tried to pull my glove off. The whole time I tried to show him that I had already prepared for that, but his eyes were closed.

After the minister pronounced us husband and wife and told Clebe he could kiss his bride, Aunt Gee-Gee, my matron of honor, and Susan Shaw, my maid of honor, stepped forward and raised my veil, carefully turning it back. I looked at Clebe. He looked at me. The audience chuckled.

Clebe whispered, "I'm not gonna kiss ya in front of six hundred people! Let's go!"

There was no use making a scene at the altar. We turned and walked down the aisle to the smiles of our friends. Clebe's convertible awaited us at the bottom of the steps outside, but the top was down.

"Clebe, I'll lose my veil if you don't put the top up."

"I'm not puttin' the top up now. Let's go!"

"I am not riding to the reception in that convertible with the top down, Clebe. I'll just ride with Daddy."

He looked at me sternly.

"You ride with your daddy, and you can just go home with him."

Just thirty seconds after our vows, we had our first argument! I rode with Clebe and hung on to veil and gown. And husband. (Clebe jokes that he won that one but not many since then!)

Clebe was impatient at the reception. He was tired of standing around.

"I've never been on a honeymoon before, and I'm ready to get goin'!"

Our honeymoon was an experience. We stayed at my Uncle Sam's Holiday Inn in Camden. Just after Clebe carried me across the threshold, he heard a familiar voice. My cousin, J. B. Lovett, had driven over to see us. Clebe ran him off, but I felt sorry for J. B. and wondered how Clebe could be so gruff with someone who had come a long way because he loved us and apparently had a need to be with us.

Clebe told me I didn't know a practical joke when I saw one and that any more than two on a honeymoon night was a crowd. We enjoyed a room service steak dinner, just the two of us.

I wanted to present myself to my husband as a gift. I had kept myself pure and that made this night so much more special, something to be anticipated and cherished. I don't know what there is to look forward to on a honeymoon if the partners have already slept with someone else or even with each other.

I had a beautiful negligee, but it took a long time to put it on because Aunt Gee-Gee, the one I had entrusted with my suitcase to protect it from pranksters, sewed up every undergarment I owned. I had to sit in the bathroom painstakingly removing the hundreds of stitches from every arm and leg hole of my underwear.

When I made my grand entrance, Clebe was on the floor

in his pajama bottoms doing pushups. Trying to look macho, I guess.

Among the first things I had to adjust to was that while at rest, especially while sleeping, Clebe's heart rate slows to about half that of a normal human being's. When he lies on his stomach, his powerful heart beats about thirty-four times a minute—probably due to all his running—and each beat shakes the bed. You can literally hear and feel his heart beating.

"Clebe! Can't you stop your heart from beating!"

"Golly, Dea, I hope not!"

"I can't sleep! I'm getting seasick! At least sleep on your back!"

He did, until I fell asleep. First thing the next morning, he popped out of bed at about five-thirty and took off on a five-mile jog. Then he was ready for a big breakfast. I really enjoyed that one with him; I especially remember the blueberry pancakes. We met friends and associates of his as we drove through the South, and it was good to get acquainted as husband and wife. I enjoyed the last few days of our honeymoon best because we spent them at the beach house at Crescent Beach. That was familiar territory, people we both knew, and more like home. Then it was on to Quantico to set up housekeeping for the first time.

CHAPTER 11

Quantico Fiascoes

*L*eaving for our honeymoon had been fun and not emotional, but when we had pulled away from Florence with a loaded U-Haul trailer to head for our first real home, I fought the tears.

By the time we stopped for gas, I was crying freely. Within a few minutes my mother drove up with items we'd forgotten, and my secret was out. I was homesick. It wasn't that I wanted to go back; in fact, I was happy to be leaving. But I wasn't as brave as I had pretended, and I dearly loved my family.

The unloading in Quantico set me up with a bunch of little friends who became almost constant companions with Clebe gone so much. Kids from the neighborhood had flocked to see who the new couple was, and in my typical way I immediately enlisted their help. We had adorable youngsters carrying wedding gifts in every door, and when they were finished, I gave them treats and got to know them. "Deanna and her band of children" became the joke of the area. We loved one another. I played with them, sang with them, traded stories with them, and even got them to help me with housework, that is, until their mothers found out. They told the kids that if they wanted to do housework, they could do it at home. I know it wasn't as much fun for them; it never is.

More than once Clebe's and my meals were interrupted when a child came to see if Lieutenant McClary's wife could "come out and play." Clebe told me it was all right as long as the kids who came to the door were younger than I was!

I had great fun decorating our new place, but I also learned a lesson about Clebe's decorating style. He's totally practical, exclusively functional. While I fixed our bedroom like a cozy honeymoon suite, he rooted around in our extra bedroom, which he had designated as his office. I went in to see how he was doing and noticed one of his favorite duck paintings hanging near the ceiling.

"Clebe, what is that doing up there?"

"Well, I found a nail there, and I figured I might as well use it. Ducks fly high, don't they?"

On our honeymoon Clebe and I had treated ourselves to a wedding present, a dog we named Easter. Our little beagle was not—of course—housebroken, so I left him in the bathroom most of the time. I didn't like the little messes he made all over the place, but both Clebe and I loved him to death. Once when we were gone for the day, we mistakenly left the bathroom door open. Easter got hold of the end of the new tissue roll and pulled the entire length throughout the apartment.

Finding creative ways to turn our apartment into a home came naturally to me. But there were also many mundane tasks involved in getting settled. Clebe gave me money for a deposit on our telephone, so I headed out in the car to get that errand done. I didn't realize that officers like Clebe had decals on their cars, signifying their rank. I didn't know why so many passing motorists and pedestrians saluted me, but I thought it was the only polite thing to salute them back! They must have thought *I* was an officer, too.

When I discovered that the phone deposit was ten more dollars than Clebe had given me, I hardly thought twice about skipping the phone for the moment and spending the money elsewhere. Our floors were spit shined to a high gloss finish, and although we couldn't afford to have them carpeted, I thought throw rugs would look darling. I chose several of different colors and surprised Clebe with them when he arrived home for dinner.

Boy, did I surprise him!

He came in, stepped on one, and nearly crashed sliding across the floor. He called my purchases "break-your-neck" rugs. He'd like to have broken my neck for buying them, and not just because they were dangerous.

"How much were these?"

I told him.

"Where'd you get the money?"

"Oh, I didn't have enough for the phone, so I used what I had for the rugs."

When he cooled down after supper, he tried to instruct me in the ways of budget planning, spending, and so forth. I could see he was losing patience with me, and it made me frantic. I tried to learn, because he was older and I knew he was right. He had a knack I didn't have for getting along in the world. I felt like Lucy Ricardo on the "I Love Lucy" show.

I spent a lot of time at Housing, where the furniture was ordered and stored. I thought it would be good to get to know people there. I complained a lot about the tacky furniture we had, and one day a load of really nice furniture was delivered to us. Clebe was scared. He knew a lieutenant didn't rate furniture of that quality, so he figured it was a mistake. He was right. We found it had been intended for a major or a general, but for some reason it was never taken back.

I had lived a sheltered life up to that point. My mother dialed long distance calls for me and drove me most anywhere I needed to go. I did girl-type things, and I worked hard when helping Daddy, but basically, I was protected. I didn't know how to cook much, and being in charge of my own household, small as it was, was intimidating.

Clebe gently advised me that his system was getting a little bound up with all the grilled cheese sandwiches I served him. I was hurt, but I wanted so badly to be a good wife that I decided to go to the commissary and find a good roast to cook him. When I got there, I noticed several highly decorated officers near the meat cases with printouts and notebooks. I decided the one with the most stars on his shoulders must be the top meat inspector, so I approached him.

"I'm sure you can tell me what would be the best cut of

meat for me to cook my husband. We're newlyweds, and I want it to be extra special nice."

He looked nonplused but flattered.

"Well, sure, ma'am. I think this roast would be very nice."

"Thank you very much."

I had to wait until Clebe got home that day to learn how to light the gas stove. He said, "Just hold a match to the little hole where it says 'ignite.'"

That sounded simple enough. The only problem was, I had turned the dial before I had asked him, assuming the oven would kick on automatically, the way the burners did on the top of the stove. I searched through the cupboard and located a book of matches, then opened the oven door and poked my head in to search for the ignition hole. There it was. I struck the match and felt my back slam against the kitchen wall eight feet from the oven.

I was speechless as Clebe howled. When I could manage to speak, I let him have it.

"How can you laugh when I could have been killed? My hair is singed. My eyebrows and eyelashes are singed. That could have burned my face off! I'm never lighting that thing again. You want anything cooked in the oven, *you* light it!"

I was serious. I never got close to that oven with a match again as long as we lived there.

Clebe enjoyed the roast, and I was thrilled to tell him how the top meat inspector had helped me.

"Meat inspector? That meat would have been inspected long before it hit this base. What did he look like?"

I told him.

"What kind of uniform?"

I told him.

"How many stars on his shoulder?"

I told him.

He paled.

"Dea, honey, I think you asked the commandant of the base for advice on beef."

"Is that bad?"

He nodded.

"If he associates me with you, he might wonder whether I know who's who around here, too."

Clebe's fear was confirmed at a reception a week later when the commandant mentioned that he had "helped your wife pick out a piece of meat for you." Clebe just about died.

One thing I both loved and hated about Clebe during those early months was his devotion to God. I had become a hit-and-miss, lackadaisical church attender, going when Daddy was Sunday school superintendent and staying home to read the paper and have a big breakfast half the time when he wasn't. As a married woman, I didn't want anybody telling me I had to go to church every Sunday, especially if I didn't feel like it.

Clebe always went. Often I pleaded with him to stay home with me.

"We'll have breakfast in bed and read the paper together."

"You can if you want, Dea. I'm goin'."

That made me furious, but I'm sure glad he never gave in to me. I would have lost respect for him. Half the time I didn't go with him. He always prayed before our meals, and most every day he read from the Bible, too. I believed he was a truly spiritual Christian.

He was also, as always, a physical fitness nut. Even with all the grueling training he received, he was a jogger. I encouraged other wives to jog with me so we could stay in shape, too. Clebe always figured I'd be at the head of the pack when he and his buddies saw a band of women jogging through the compound.

One day while running, I noticed a hillside covered with gorgeous flowers. When we finished running, I showered and changed and went back to pick a handful. They made a beautiful centerpiece for our candlelight dinner that night. Clebe was impressed.

"Pretty. Where'd you get 'em?"

"On that hill on the north side."

Clebe's sigh blew out one of the candles.

"You've got a lot to learn, girl. There's a general's house at the top of that hill, and those were his flowers."

I couldn't win!

Clebe missed the kind of cooking he'd grown up with, so after a weekend home, I came back with frozen game fowl his daddy had shot. I also had his mother's cookbook. For a feast for several officers, I cooked up a duck with all the trimmings, stuffing, the whole bit. When I brought the bursting bird to the table, Clebe jumped up and took it directly to the kitchen. I was confused, but I covered for him.

"He's carving."

But he didn't return for a while, and I heard strange noises from the kitchen. He brought back the duck, but it appeared two-thirds its original size. And it was still whole.

"You didn't carve it?"

"Oh, you can do that, honey."

"Clebe, uh, what did you do with my dressing?"

"Dressing? At home we always put the dressing in the bowl, not in the wrong end of the duck! I thought you'd forgotten to clean the bird."

I was sure he was kidding, and I went into the kitchen to find the bowl he'd dumped my dressing in. But he had held that steaming duck in his bare hands and shaken it over the garbage pail. For once, he had been the goofy one. I didn't think it was funny. I was glad I had prepared a large dessert.

We had been in Quantico nearly three months when I had a physical trauma that nearly scared me to death and could have literally killed me. I had been prescribed birth control pills just before we got married because my monthly cycle was due during our honeymoon. I was told that the pills would delay or make me skip my time of the month and not complicate our honeymoon.

It was so great to go a month without a problem that I kept taking the pills. I skipped two more months, but of course it caught up with me. I awoke in the middle of the night, having terrible cramps and hemorrhaging in such great clots that it was as if I were having a miscarriage. I was scared and confused. This was the first time I'd been ill away from home. Clebe called my mother, who told him what to do.

He applied ice packs and called the doctor, who prescribed some medicine. I pulled through without much trouble except for a tremendous loss of blood, but I sure learned a lesson about birth control pills.

I should have known better. Despite my sheltered upbringing, I was familiar with medical things, and I had even started back to college at Mary Washington in Fredericksburg, Virginia. I came home to Quantico from school one afternoon to a ringing phone. It was a major I had always found condescending and obnoxious.

"Mrs. McClary, did you feed your husband breakfast this morning?"

"No, sir, I didn't. I . . ."

"And why did you not feed him breakfast?"

"He didn't want to eat before the PRT [Physical Readiness Test]. He had the PRT today."

"I'm well aware of that, ma'am. He's in intensive care at the base hospital right now with a fever of 108 as the result of severe heat stroke."

I didn't even pause to let it sink in that I was being blamed because of failing to serve Clebe breakfast. What was I supposed to do, force-feed a grown man? I dropped the phone and raced to the hospital. Clebe was sitting up in bed, conscious but pale and weak looking. He tried to make light of it, but I knew it embarrassed him. He was a strong, athletic man who took great pride in his endurance. He had been running the three-mile in full gear on a day when such tests shouldn't even have been held. He told me the finish line had begun to swim away from him at about the three-hundred-yard mark, and he had fallen twice and been doused with canteen water once before passing out.

Because a couple of other guys had passed out that day, an ambulance was on the scene. If it hadn't been for the massive strength of Clebe's heart, he might not have survived. He had been unconscious for almost an hour without so much as a twitching muscle.

A medic told me that the only time Clebe almost came to was when they first immersed his body in ice.

"He was moaning, ma'am."

"Oh, my dear Clebe. Was he calling for me? Was he saying, 'Deanna'?"

"No, ma'am. What he said was more like, 'Gung ho, gung ho, I love the Marine Corps.'"

Of all the nerve!

Clebe was worried about that test because it was compulsory for further duty. Fortunately, there were no long-lasting effects, but he was eliminated from the football program, which would have kept him from Vietnam into the late fall season schedule.

When you've suffered from heat stroke, your internal thermostat can be permanently affected. Clebe could have petitioned to get out of going to Vietnam, where the tropical forests can wreak havoc on the normal body cooling system. For someone who has shown low tolerance to heat and humidity—the temperature at Quantico that day was near 100 degrees with the humidity at 98 percent (much like the temperature and humidity in Vietnam)—such a climate could be deadly.

I pleaded with Clebe to take advantage of what I saw as a break. It was a scary, dangerous, life-threatening break, and ironically it pushed him toward Vietnam earlier because of precluding him from football. That seemed crazy to me. He couldn't play football, but he could risk his life on the front lines?

"Clebe, just say the word—tell them you have a wife and want to start a family—and you'll never have to go. You have a definite medical waiver now. Use it!"

I might as well have been talking to the wall.

I wanted Clebe to be a good Marine, and I wanted him to do well in all his training. Besides the fact that I just wanted to be proud of my husband, I didn't know whether he'd wind up in combat, but just in case I wanted him ready.

I listened when he told me which guys were sharp in mapping and positioning and logistics, because that was a tough area for him. Then I invited them over and told them I would fix them a good southern home-cooked meal if they'd help Clebe study. I stuck to the simple things until I learned to cook better, but it always seemed a good deal for both sides. I was gratified years later to learn that one of the things Clebe's men respected most in him was his ability to chart their position in the jungle. I'd like to think I had something to do with keeping him—and his men—alive.

I also learned the parts of the M-14 rifle and could probably have physically torn one down myself if I'd been forced to. I called out each part to Clebe, reminded him of the name, shape, and function, and walked him through that operation time and time again. It's crucial that men in combat know their weapons intimately and be able to take them apart and put them back together. Clebe became an expert. Of course, he already knew how to shoot, and the jungle wouldn't be much different from the ten-thousand-acre Friendfield Plantation where he grew up.

The major issue I had to deal with as a new wife was that I didn't know what my role was. Clebe was so independent, so schooled in the ways of society and the world—and certainly the military—that all I was there for was to serve him and learn to grow up. That, needless to say, did little for my sense of self-worth.

Because I felt alone, like an outsider, I forced myself into his business. I tried to advise him how to deal with his military career. I didn't get far with that, but I was successful in making him a better student of war.

My biggest problem was that I felt Clebe isolated me from his feelings. He married me, then he got on with his life. He was still loving and kind and compassionate and considerate— at least as far as he knew the meanings of those words—but he never let me in on his worries or frustrations. He didn't tell me how tough things were or how scared he was or how depressing military life could be. He had done that when we were engaged, but once we were married, I wouldn't have known he had a problem in the world.

Clebe worried he would be kicked out because of his collapse; that's why he shouted all that gung ho Marine stuff. And for some reason he seemed bound for Vietnam, regardless of the options that could have prevented his going. Perhaps he felt a call, a date with destiny. I don't know.

Clebe would have appeared even more masculine to me if he had displayed some vulnerability. That would have seemed a show of weakness to him, but without it, I didn't know my place. I needed to know that he hurt and had fears. There were problems in his life that only I could solve, but I didn't get the chance.

I longed to be his salve, his solvent, his solace, his bandage. I wanted to be a helpmeet, a helpmate, not just a playmate. All Clebe thought about was combat, competition, sports, ducks, quail, deer, guns, everything but me. My competition was not other women. He wasn't any more concerned or interested in them than he was in me. My competition was the outdoors and Clebe's fierce independence.

He wasn't doing this to me on purpose; I knew that. I wanted to reach him, but I didn't know how. I didn't know my purpose in the marriage, and I couldn't for the life of me figure out why he had married me. I felt very insecure. Why had he fallen in love with me? All day, every day, I did everything to solidify his love for me, but there's no hiding the insecure spouse's clawing, clutching, possessive ways.

He was determined that I learn to do everything he did, and so I became a sort of tomboy for a long time. Doing womanly, wifely things went by the board as I learned to hike and trail and hunt and fish and participate in sports. It was all right with me—anything to be near him. But I wasn't being myself either. Something was out of whack. I became involved in his life to the absolute exclusion of any of the things I thought I might like to do.

I can't say I didn't enjoy it or that I didn't learn a lot. I went from being an uninformed spendthrift who spent the phone money on break-your-neck rugs to a woman who hunted for a bargain until the sun went down. Still, I felt

Clebe could have found someone older, smarter, more independent, someone with something to offer him in life. I was like a little sister who had to tag along and be either taught everything or tolerated.

I wanted a bigger stake in his life, but I didn't know how to get it.

CHAPTER *12*

Such Sweet
Sorrow

I was so proud of Clebe I could hardly stand it. He had distinguished himself as a tough Marine officer candidate, and he was now a second lieutenant. The academic part of the training had been the toughest for him, and early on he had worked hard to bring up his average to be eligible to play football. His heat stroke ended that anyway.

The day his orders came through was one of the saddest of my life. Those orders read like an itinerary through hell: Charleston to Atlanta to Dallas to San Francisco. At Travis Air Force Base Clebe would walk proudly beneath a sign that read: "Through this door march the world's greatest men."

One of the world's greatest men would fly from there to Hawaii—with no time even to leave the airport—and then on to Okinawa for final processing before entering Vietnam at Da Nang.

I grieved as I sat looking at those orders. My idyllic honeymoon life was over. I wished I hadn't become such a nag. I wished I'd gotten to know Clebe better, to not let him shut me out, to push my way into the recesses of his mind and heart and soul and convince him—and myself—that I was necessary in his life.

I had a lot to offer him. I was unflagging in my love and devotion and loyalty, yet I sensed that to him I was just his little girl. I didn't want the spotlight; in fact, I wanted a behind-the-scenes role. I just wanted him to make full use of my abilities. I could complement him, round him out, challenge him intellectually, make a fantastic man into a Renaissance man, if he'd let me.

We had about a week to ourselves before he had to leave, so we stationed ourselves at his parents' home and traveled all over the area for his farewells to our families and all his friends. Then Clebe did something unexpected. For the last few days before the trip to Charleston, he isolated us from everyone and devoted his time to me.

That time was short-lived, melancholy, and gloomy in its anticipation, but also heavenly. It wasn't just that I had him to myself; more than that, it had been his idea. He needed to solidify our relationship, to strengthen our bond for the lonely days ahead. It was an incredibly romantic time, the memories of which have lasted a lifetime. We embraced, we cuddled, we kissed, we walked, we talked, we loved each other.

I tried not to talk about my dread of his future. I forbade any negative talk. Boy friends, lovers, and husbands were shipped back dead from Vietnam. Everyone knew that. This wasn't like World War II when almost every family had someone involved and we were all in it together. Vietnam was a maddening, solitary struggle that split the nation. The war was controversial. People in the South were as patriotic as any, and they were proud Clebe was going out of a sense of duty. But there was an undercurrent of pity, too. It was as if people were saying it was too bad a fine young man like Clebe had to have his honor tested and maybe wasted in such a futile conflict.

Clebe didn't feel that way. He believed the U.S. was in Vietnam to stop the spread of communism, to defend innocent lives, and to maintain our powerful military position in the eyes of friend and foe alike. He was eager to go, to use his skills, to test his endurance, to show that a plantation-born and-bred country boy was made for just such a war.

He wouldn't deny that he was also afraid. He had never been outside the United States. He'd never shot at anyone or been shot at. He knew that even the most savvy outdoorsman, the most rugged athlete, could be killed in an instant halfway around the world through no fault of his own. I tried often during those precious few days to look deep into his eyes. I read love there, love for me, for his parents, for relatives on both sides. I also read longing, fear, a sense that the time was passing too quickly, as it was for me.

My plan was to live at home again, take up my nursing courses, and model at Hendrickson's, a dress shop, generally trying to keep as busy as possible. Clebe and I agreed to write every day. Amazingly, he would keep up his end of the bargain, and when we began sending cassette tapes back and forth, he was faithful in that, too.

For weeks I replayed in my mind the scene at the Charleston airport on October 8, 1967, when Clebe traced "I love you" on the window next to his seat on the plane. The bright sunshine and crisp temperatures were too cheery for the occasion. I wouldn't allow myself to consider never seeing him again, but that fear was no harbored secret. The question of whether Clebe would come back alive was a raging monster that growled and screamed and roared at me every waking moment. It was in the eyes of all the people who asked about him, encouraged me, or said they were praying for us.

Clebe's safety was the first thing I thought about when I awoke every morning and the last thing I thought about before drifting off to sleep. Of course, I dreamed about him, too.

Clebe's mother and I got a map of Vietnam, and every day we carefully plotted where Clebe was. From news reports and his letters, I was able to project myself into his life, following him through the jungles and valleys, and as much as was possible from halfway around the world, I was there with him. While the rest of the country seemed to try to forget Vietnam, to put the ugly war out of its mind, I plotted, planned, lived through it. My heart was there.

I wrote and asked Clebe why a certain valley was called Happy Valley. He told me it was because the guys were so happy to get out of there alive. The Leech Valley was so named because of the painful leech bites the men suffered. They couldn't scream or moan or even grunt for fear of bringing enemy fire on themselves. And removing leeches by hand meant removing some of your own skin in the process.

The plan was for Clebe to be in Vietnam for a thirteen-month tour, but when he was slightly wounded during the Tet offensive between Christmas and New Year's and won a Purple Heart, his rest and recuperation schedule was moved up to March, almost a year since we'd been married.

Clebe grew up as soon as he got to Vietnam. One of the first men he met came back the next day with his legs blown off. When Clebe was introduced to the general in charge of the First Marine Division, he was told that the most pressing need was for lieutenants in recon. Clebe saw this as a matter of honor. He was needed. He hadn't had the special training, but he had been raised with a great understanding of the outdoors. He forgot his promise to me and answered in the only way consistent with his character. He thought country, duty, and patriotism first, Clebe last. Unfortunately, that put me last, too. Frustrated as I was with him, what could I do? There may have been safer jobs and places in Vietnam, but there were no guarantees. Cooks and medics came back in boxes, too.

The survivors of the recon platoon called "Texas Pete"—in which the man had lost his legs—became the nucleus of Clebe's unit. Helicopters flew him and his men to the mountains behind enemy lines to survey Viet Cong (VC) troop movement and gather information on their locations. (Recon platoons played hide-and-seek with the enemy behind their lines, trying to figure out where the Viet Cong were, where U.S. troops could advance and attack, and how to keep areas clear of booby traps and mines.) The goal was to come up with as much valuable information as possible in a four-to twenty-six day period without engaging the enemy.

Clebe's unit was a part of First Recon, which was always a step or two from death. There were times they could hear the VC talking, even breathing. When detection could not be avoided, First Recon was forced to fight their way out and radio for helicopter evacuation.

Clebe told me that most recon teams either completed their missions safely or were badly wounded. There was rarely any middle ground. Recon units avoided contact as much as possible, but when they had to, they fought.

When the news came of his small facial wound, which—the message said—was minor enough to allow him to continue in action, I was frantic. I cried for days, worried that I hadn't been told the whole story. There were even rumors, which I believed in spite of myself, that he had been killed. His letters continued uninterrupted, so I knew he was alive. But why hadn't he told me about the injury? How had it happened? Why couldn't he be sent home?

When I demanded by letter and tape that Clebe tell me what had happened, he reminded me that he had wanted to train for recon duty, but that there hadn't been enough time for the additional schooling. How well I remembered that. I had considered it an answer to prayer and made Clebe promise to never seek such suicide duty again.

Clebe explained his facial wound in such a way that it really did seem minor. He wasn't even aware he had been hurt until he discovered blood later, but in the account of the skirmish that caused it, he scared me senseless. He had faced the enemy head-on and had killed a few of them, then was pinned down by thirty or so shots from an AK-47, an automatic weapon. He thought he had evaded the fire, though shrapnel and stones and sticks exploded all around him. A few minutes later he noticed blood coming from his nose. That earned him what he considered an embarrassing Purple Heart. He kidded that if he could get himself two more such medals, he could come home. The odds were astronomical against a man earning three Purple Hearts and coming home alive.

I was relieved to hear that the injury was minor, but the story of the fight itself was alarming. I had hoped against hope that Clebe's recon unit would be lucky, that they would scout out areas and encampments without being detected. To think of Clebe being close enough to the VC to shoot and kill them and to be pinned down and shot in the face by one of them graphically brought home to me exactly what he was into.

I lived in terror from day to day, waiting for news of his death. I tried to keep busy and appear brave, but I was losing the battle. Frankly, I was surprised every day the news came that he was still fine. I bided my time, pleading with God to keep him safe until March when we could be together in Hawaii. If I could just see him, touch him, hold him, I would be whole again. The closer the days drew toward our rendezvous, the more I allowed myself a shred of confidence. I couldn't let my guard down and jump to any conclusions. I couldn't assume the best. The only advantage Clebe had now was that he had fewer days to be vulnerable to the impersonal fates of war.

Two months before he was hit, in a letter dated January 6, 1968, Clebe wrote:

> Don't read the papers. They always tell the worst. I
> am fine and am enjoying the beautiful countryside and
> many colorful birds, monkeys, and apes we run across.
> I'd like to get a book on the birds in the jungles of
> Vietnam. They are really unbelievable.

I knew that every day in Vietnam, especially for the leader of a recon unit, could be a date with death. In a letter dated 5:00 A.M., February 27, 1968, six days before my twentieth birthday, Clebe wrote,

> My dearest Deanna,
> We had a break in the weather about 5 P.M.
> yesterday and saw the sun for the first time in 15 days.
> Tried to get out but couldn't get a chopper to come in
> after us. I'm really tired of Nam and this watch every
> night in the wind and rain is really getting me and my
> men down. We all want a shower, shave, clean clothes,
> hot chow, and *most* of all, mail!
> Just think, darling, by the time you get this letter
> it will be just fourteen days till we're together in

Hawaii. Isn't it going to be great? Just like getting married all over again. I love you more and more each day and since coming to Nam have had so much time to think, dream, and just glow all over when I think how lucky I am to be married to the most wonderful girl in the world.

Corporal Munoz is going to be married in Hawaii. You should hear us as we just sit all day and talk about it. We both say we aren't going to sleep for seven days in Hawaii and if our wives fall asleep, we'll just go surfing by ourselves. Munoz is a great boy; you will really like him. He doesn't have that long to serve and wants to get out.

So far I've gotten all my married men promoted because they need all the money they can save. I don't have but five married men in my platoon.

Hope all the family is well. Please give them my best. If Daddy won't come with Mother, why not get your mother to come with her? They could be together and you and I can be together.

Tell Jennie and Annette hey and give them a big kiss for me. Give my best to Dean but don't kiss him for me.

I love you the mostest. Clebe.

P.S. Dea, check list for me in Hawaii. Please bring:

1. Dea
2. Mother
3. Daddy
4. Camera
5. Underwater housing [scuba equipment]
6. Film
7. Flash bulbs
8. Diving cord
9. Swimsuit
10. Lightweight suit/shirt/tie (old type from home)

11. Jim Ryun story
12. How to Become a Champion
13. Counting your plane fare and *our* (me and you) expenses, total will be close to $1000. I hope to have half of this if I can get in to get paid.
14. All your LOVE!
15. Any slides I haven't seen

That evening, at 8:30, he wrote his parents:

> Dear Mother and Daddy,
> Got in tonight to some bad news. Pfc. Ragsdale—who just got back from seeing his wife and six-month-old son on R & R in Hawaii—went on a patrol with Cowpoke, another platoon. A bunker caved in and crushed his chest and skull. He was clinically dead for ten minutes before they revived him and got him medivaced out. I saw him today. He's still in a coma with a 50–50 chance of pulling through. He is a very good boy and it really hurts to see this happen.
> Also hope to call you all tomorrow night. Plan to leave on 16 March for R & R and will be there until 22 March. Only one more patrol to sweat and then I'll be with you and Dea!
> All my love, Clebe.

And at 9:00 he wrote,

> Dearest Deanna,
> Well, got back to base camp today and welcomed mail from you and home. Was greeted with bad news. . . .
> Darling, the only times I can call from over here will be in the mornings. I will be in the bush next Saturday and Sunday, so I'm going to try and catch Mother or Daddy home tomorrow.
> Got my new track shoes. They are very pretty and

feel great. Ran five miles in them today.

Well, darling, I'm going to hit the rack. Feels like I haven't slept in two months.

All my love, Clebe.

I couldn't know how ironic and ominous those two innocuous sentences would appear later:

"Only one more patrol to sweat. . . ."

"I will be in the bush next Saturday and Sunday. . . ."

Indeed.

I didn't know that on my twentieth birthday, despite my wish before blowing out the candles, Clebe's destiny was decided. In a half-dozen ways for twice as many reasons he should have been killed or left for dead. Here, reconstructed from his account and the testimonies of others I corresponded with in his unit, is what happened March 3, 1968, in the Quan Duc Valley, thirty miles south of Da Nang.

Clebe's nineteenth patrol with the First Marine Division's First Reconnaissance Battalion was designed to pave the way for an attack involving several thousand troops. They would land on Hill 146, which another recon team had surveyed months earlier. A few days before Clebe's platoon got there, U.S. planes warned civilians with loudspeakers and leaflets that they were on the way so the civilians would not be hurt. However, if the North Vietnamese army got wind of the plan, the enemy troops would either evacuate or set up the strongest defense possible.

Just before Clebe's recon unit dropped in, U.S. planes shelled the area to detonate booby traps. As U.S. helicopters neared the ground, their powerful rotor blades whipped up the dust and revealed three box mines, several booby traps, and a pungi (pun' gee) pit. These pits were about four feet by six feet and six feet deep. They were covered with a bamboo mat, which was then camouflaged with foliage. It was a good thing they were exposed because the wires led down one side of the hill to detonators with enemy probably at the ready to blow up the choppers as soon as they landed.

One of Clebe's men, Pfc. Tom Jennings, leaped from a chopper and cut the wires, finding one of the box mines a dud and the other two live. Had the enemy known he was cutting the wires, they could have triggered the mechanism and killed him. As it was, he made it safe for the rest to land.

Clebe helped set mines, booby traps, and flares, then cleared the pungi pit himself. Had the chopper not exposed it and had a Marine stepped on it, he would have fallen into the pit onto bamboo sticks sharpened like razors and covered with human waste. By the time a soldier was extracted, if he could be at all, infection would have set in.

Within an hour, Clebe's conspicuous and tension-filled men had cleared the area, dug themselves foxholes, and set up protection in the crater made by a huge bomb. Clebe felt he had his men in the best fighting position ever. Soon the Cong in the valley let the Marines know they were there. They chanted and beat sticks and occasionally fired off a sniping round. One narrowly missed Clebe. He called in artillery to shell the area, but still his men could do nothing to draw attention to themselves. They had to speak in whispers, keep their exposed skin blackened, and stay awake at night.

The operation scheduled for the valley was canceled, and Clebe's platoon was scheduled to be helicoptered out. But bad weather kept the choppers away, and the men, socked in, grew restless. An eerie silence settled on their position as they waited . . . and waited . . . and waited. An occasional rocket signaled a potential attack. Clebe consulted his top assistants. Every avenue of escape was ruled out, except air, and until the weather cleared, that was really no option.

Although their primary task was to survey and hide, hiding became impossible. They would have to stay and endure the unknown, at least until the chopper pilots could see through the clouds and rain.

The third night, darkness fell hot and humid and deathly still, save for the sounds of insects. Every man was on alert, no one sleeping. Hour after hour they waited, sensing the enemy was upon them but not knowing from which direction the VC might attack.

Fatigue could not dent the suspense as every man listened. Each thought of his loved ones, of the weather, of the choppers, of the impending attack, of his chances. This was their destiny, what they had trained for, what they had dreaded.

Clebe's position was in a little shelf at the the top of the pungi pit. Cleared, it was no longer dangerous and afforded him a superior vantage point. He trusted his men, and they loved and trusted him. Several wrote me later, extolling his character and bravery and intelligence in the jungle. They exulted over his ability to draw them together, to cross-train everyone so that no matter who was hurt or killed, someone else knew his job.

At about midnight, Clebe thought he heard rustling at the bottom of the hill. Was it just his imagination? Had the others heard it, too? Moving might give away his position, but not checking with the others might be suicidal.

There it was again. Were the VC moving or talking? He had to know. He crept out of the pit and then to his right where three of his men huddled in a foxhole. Before he could speak to them, a grenade exploded nearby, and white hot shrapnel slashed into his neck and shoulder. He dropped and rolled, then dove back into the pungi pit, no longer worried about silence.

He screamed into his radio, seeking artillery and air support for their position. Poking his head out of the pit, he saw the sky lit by explosions. VC charged up the hill with grenades in their hands and satchel charges tied to their belts. They were suicide squads, blowing themselves up as they hurled themselves at the recon team. The only hope was to shoot the exploding Cong before they got close enough to blow up everyone at once.

Where was safety? Outside the pit, dozens of VC stormed the hill. One got through the fire and towered above Clebe. With his shotgun Clebe got off the first shot. The VC lurched forward, falling, probably already dead. He fell into the pit with Clebe, a pouch filled with self-detonating charges on his belt.

CHAPTER 13

Itinerary through Hell

*T*he satchel charges exploded and threw Clebe and the dead VC through the air. Clebe scrambled back for his shotgun and reached for it but came up empty. He turned and saw it, but his arm wasn't functioning. Then he saw why.

His left arm, just below the elbow, was just a bloody stump. He lay stunned, thoughts flooding his mind. *Was the end near? Would he and his entire platoon be wiped out?* He prayed for the nightmare to end, but a scream brought him back to action. A live grenade had landed in the foxhole to his right.

Ralph Johnson, a black Pfc. from Charleston, South Carolina, fell on the grenade and was killed, saving the lives of his comrades. To Clebe's left, a radio man and corpsman lay unconscious, bleeding from gaping wounds. He grabbed his shotgun with his right hand and raced to the bomb crater. Five were wounded, and the enemy kept coming. It was kill or be killed. He put a grenade to his mouth and attempted to bite the pin. Impossible. His teeth had been shattered in the first explosion.

His only hope now was to run from position to position, trying to bolster the few remaining men and direct their fire. Another grenade flew past his head. He covered his face with—he thought—both hands, pressing them against his eyes. He didn't realize that he had only phantom feeling in his left arm and that the grenade had shattered all his teeth, blown out his left eye, and ripped his face open from forehead to chin right through the nose. His missing left hand had been of no protection. The right hand that had saved his right eye was diced by the shrapnel, bones and tendons exposed, useless. He gagged on bits of teeth and burning gums. He was blinded by blood.

Every nerve ending recorded the sounds of screaming, of grenades and bombs exploding, of small weapon fire. Clebe was aware of his own heart, his breathing. His eardrums had been perforated. He saw himself imprisoned by torture with no escape.

His men were falling on every side. He wanted to live! He wanted *them* to live! His only hope was the bomb crater. He dove for it. As he tumbled in, yet another grenade slid between his knees and ripped apart his legs.

Blind save for one bloodied eye, one remaining hand in shreds, legs useless, he lay motionless, knowing only from the pain that he was even still alive. The movement near him could be only VC, so he pretended to be dead. An enemy soldier bent over Clebe and leveled his weapon on Clebe's head.

Another time, another place, another circumstance, and Clebe would have called on every self-defense mechanism built into him. He would have taken the weapon, killed the enemy, regained his position. But all his resources were gone. His men were dead or dying. He fought to remain still, hoping the Cong would decide not to waste the bullet on him. He still heard only confusing sounds, but the flash of light next to his face told him the weapon had been fired. His body lurched and lay still again. He felt the sharp pain in his neck and the blood oozing toward his back. There was some grim satisfaction that the enemy couldn't even accomplish a kill shot to the brain from point-blank range. Then he saw the VC drop, obviously hit just before he had fired. But by whom?

Suddenly Clebe was alone. He couldn't move. He couldn't see. Had the enemy left? Where was the survivor who had shot the VC? More movement behind him no doubt. Pfc.

Rod Hunter called out to Clebe, but Clebe couldn't respond. He had to wait until Hunter moved into his sight to assure him he was still alive. Hunter knelt by Clebe's feet and shot the enemy one by one as they came over the hill.

Clebe shouted, though he could barely hear himself.

"Take over the patrol, Hunter! Call for choppers!"

Hunter grabbed Clebe's radio.

"Texas Pete to base! Hill 146 overrun by VC! Need choppers to evacuate!"

The reply angered Hunter.

"Negative till daybreak, Texas Pete! Rain and fog!"

"Forget it! Nobody will be left by dawn!"

Ten of Clebe's thirteen men were dead or wounded, but for some reason the enemy had regrouped at the bottom of the hill. They could have easily overrun the feeble remains of Texas Pete. Meanwhile, chopper pilots flying to another mission heard Hunter's plea for help and reconsidered their course. The first helicopter picked up the dead and wounded, except Clebe. The second picked up everyone else, not realizing Clebe had been left behind. Hunter jumped out and ran to Clebe, then dragged him fifty yards to the chopper. With Clebe's legs hanging out, the copter lifted off as 150 VC stormed the hill. Thirty more seconds and every American would have been dead.

Clebe's horrific itinerary began at Marble Mountain Hospital near Da Nang—where his men visited for a last look. I didn't learn until years later how close he came to death on the hill and in that hospital, where doctors had to slap him to get a vein to bulge so they could pump blood into him.

When his memory dredges up flashes of those days and nights of torture, all he sees are tubes running in and out of his body and frantic attempts to stabilize him and keep him alive. From there he went to two hospitals in Japan, then finally to Bethesda Naval in Maryland. It was at Bethesda, while I stayed with Clebe's Uncle Dorsey and Aunt Lucille, that I took over.

I had discovered my mission in life. I was going to personally nurse Patrick Cleburn McClary III back to health. I would be whatever he needed me to be, and eventually I would not be what he *didn't* need me to be—in other words, when he got to the place where he could do for himself, I would see that he did.

At first, of course, he was merely stabilized enough that he was out of immediate danger. I say that advisedly, because a person like Clebe, wounded seven times over a short period, has shrapnel in his body that could move and become deadly in just hours. In that sense, he's always on the brink of death, even today.

But he was not going to die from the trauma inflicted on his body, short of shrapnel movement, so the task before me— though no one expected me to accept it—was to rehabilitate him. Other ailing soldiers had supportive families, including some members who spent most of every day with the patient. I spent hours with Clebe in therapy during his months at Bethesda. I lost any sense of what time of day or what day of the week it was. But time didn't matter. I say that not to boast; it's simply a fact. I loved this man. I wanted to be for him what I would have wanted him to be for me.

I knew that not many people—even those who loved him most dearly—were capable of stomaching what I had to see and do and endure. There wasn't any virtue in the fact that I felt capable and called to it. I had been born to this and for this. My difficult childhood, my nurturing and nursing instinct, my people skills, and my training all went into making me the woman I was.

I had found my niche, my calling, my life. Sure it was repugnant at times. And it wasn't all glorious and heroic. We had our bad days. But I tried to see the big picture, to look to the future, to keep everything in perspective. I knew Clebe would never again be whole. But neither was he going to be a parasite, a bitter, old, wounded veteran.

I wanted back the Clebe I had married. He would have only one eye and one arm, and the teeth would be implants, but I would let nothing dampen his spirit. I wanted my independent, outdoorsy, can-do husband back, and I would do anything in my power to make that happen. He would need me more than ever—more at first, of course. But for the rest of our lives, I would in many respects be indispensable to him. This was an awful price to pay to be needed, but I determined from the beginning that I would never hold it over his head, demean him with it, or use it against him. I would help maintain his dignity. He would become, of course, more fiercely independent than if he had been whole, yet little things—like opening jars, buttoning shirts, tying shoes—could always be done more quickly and easily with a helping hand. My hand. Unobtrusively. Lovingly.

I began by showing up at Bethesda before the sun rose. There were strict and very limited visiting hours, and Clebe was in a double room where I was considered an intruder—not by the other patient but by personnel whose job it was to major on such minors. I learned to sneak in by avoiding the main lobby and trotting up fourteen flights of stairs.

I watched until the coast was clear, then slipped into Clebe's room and sat watching him as he slept. He did not sleep well. Blood clogged his nose. His wounds oozed. Pain made him restless. Painkillers left him in a stupor. His breathing was labored, his movement excruciating. Tears welled up in my eyes as I sought to imagine his pain. At first he was so hurt and so dependent that I thought of him as my own little boy, and I loved him tenderly.

His remaining hand was ultrasensitive and fragile. It needed a lot of work, stimulation, and movement, despite the pain. As he began to stir early in the morning, I would release that hand from the bandages enough to get access to it, and I would massage it, gently at first, then more vigorously until I was kneading it, stimulating it, bringing blood and feeling and color to it. Sometimes it hurt Clebe, but he gritted his teeth and let me do it, knowing it was the only hope for the use of any fingers.

The corpsmen usually looked the other way when I was there during nonvisiting hours, because I made their jobs easier. I fed Clebe, changed his bandages, applied salves, bathed him, talked to him, read to him, listened to him. There were times, especially when nurses or doctors were scheduled to see Clebe, when I scooted back out into the hall or down to a waiting area to appear less conspicuous.

There were nurses we liked and some we didn't. The physical therapist, John Hetrick, was of tremendous encouragement to both Clebe and me. At first, Clebe saw the painful process of rehabilitation as an insurmountable ordeal. I embraced it because I clearly saw my role. I would be a cheerleader, an encourager. I would get to know John and listen and learn from him. I wanted to know everything, not just what had to be done, but also why and what results and benefits were expected.

John taught me what it was really going to take to get Clebe back on his feet: basically working with him all the time. John pushed Clebe when he didn't think he could do another leg lift, when he didn't think he could go on, when he wondered if all the pain was worth it. John assured him it was. I did the same, every chance I got. I drilled Clebe so that when he had to "perform" for his therapist, he could. It was gratifying later to hear that John Hetrick gave me a lot of credit for the quality of Clebe's recuperation, and he wasn't talking about just the physical therapy; he meant the mental and spiritual support.

I could hardly stand what I saw in occupational therapy. People with no arms, using two hooks, learned to tie neckties and make little items out of clay, all in an attempt to re-enter society able to take care of themselves. The men got angry and threw things, and I always wanted to help them. I was grateful they were able to take out their anger on inanimate objects and not on people. A lot of men who came back physically whole from Vietnam could have used occupational therapy to let their anger out.

Very few things made Clebe mad. But one nurse—whom he called the Drill Sergeant—got to him. She never smiled, never encouraged, always barked and ordered both of us around. It was partly because she didn't like me. She said I sounded like the little girl with the twangy Southern accent on the old Shake 'n Bake commercial. I probably did, but so what? I'm proud I was born and raised in the South.

One of the things we liked to do was to get out of the room as much as possible. If dinner was served downstairs, I'd ask a corpsman to help me get Clebe into a wheelchair. We'd wait till his dizziness cleared, then I would take him down and feed him. It was therapeutic for both of us. The only problem was, the Drill Sergeant made it tough on us.

"You don't leave this room without a shirt and tie, Marine."

Clebe shook his head. "I'm in my pajamas. I don't need an old tie."

She took a deep breath.

"No tie, no supper."

She made us angry, but she also made us want even more for Clebe to get well soon. In her negative, ornery, mean-spirited way, she was a motivator. I don't think she intended to be or knew she was, but she was. Although she seemed to begrudge what she was doing, she was—in her own way—an angel of mercy, a catalyst for Clebe's improvement.

One day I was sent from Clebe's room while the staff was taking care of something. I found myself idly staring out the window down the hall. I became aware that an older man stood near me. He was a large man with wide shoulders, which appeared to be stooped in turmoil. If I told him about Clebe, maybe his problem wouldn't seem so overwhelming. During the course of our conversation, he mentioned his name, but I didn't catch it. I discovered he was a retired Marine who had seen action in World War II and Korea.

"What rank?"

"General."

"Oh, please come and meet Clebe sometime. He's a lieutenant, and I know he'd love to meet a retired Marine general."

Later in the day, when the general appeared at Clebe's

door, Clebe's face lighted up.

"You're General Chesty Puller. It's an honor to meet you, sir."

General Puller—Clebe told me later he was one of the most decorated Marines ever—seemed genuinely pleased that Clebe had recognized him.

"Well, that's what they used to call me. My chest has dropped a bit these days."

He told us of his son, Lou, in the room next door, blown apart in Vietnam and confined to a Stryker frame where the entire bed is turned when the patient needs to be turned over. And we thought we had problems!

I knew Clebe and I had turned a major corner one day when we felt free enough to laugh. We were in the bathroom, and I was working with a miniature rubberized suction cup to get a marblelike ball into Clebe's empty eye socket. It was needed to prepare him for a glass eye someday, but the mechanism was giving me fits.

Once I got the ball into his eye, the suction cup was supposed to release automatically. But no matter what I did, that thing stayed on the ball. Finally, I couldn't contain myself.

"Clebe, you do look a sight!"

He looked in the mirror and laughed. "That thing looks wonderful, hangin' outta my eye!"

I laughed all the harder, then we got to teasing about what kind of eyeball he should buy. He had the best, and funniest, idea.

"How 'bout a recon glass eye? Instead of an eyeball painted on it, I'll take a skull and crossbones. That oughta get me some attention."

"Yeah. And some respect."

We were both giggling when an angry corpsman stuck his head in, prepared to scold me for laughing at my poor husband. When he got a look at Clebe with that suction thing in his eye, he had to chuckle, too.

"I think you two are gonna make it."

I laughed so hard I became weak, so the orderly had to remove the mechanism from Clebe's eye.

Unfortunately, those light moments were too few and too infrequent. Clebe underwent several operations to remove shrapnel from his legs and feet, his gums, and his head. The recuperation time for each surgery seemed to set us back that much more. The pain was intense, the discomfort agonizing. One eardrum was reconstructed using the lining of a vein in Clebe's temple. The other ear would wait until we were transferred to Philadelphia Naval Hospital.

We were getting tired of hospital life. Even after I crept out and down the stairs at one or two in the morning and got to Lucille and Dorsey's home, it seemed I could smell the hospital. My dreams were about Clebe and Bethesda. We needed to get away from there, somehow, some way, someday.

That day came when we were given permission to take Clebe to Aunt Lucille's for a day. His mother and dad came, and we planned to drive him. First Clebe had to be bathed, medicated, and bandaged more carefully than ever. They gave us myriads of instructions and warnings, cautioning us to be careful with him, to not let him overexert, and to have him back on time.

I was so excited for him I could hardly manage. I knew how freeing it would be for him to get some fresh air, to get away from the hospital atmosphere, to be able to visit casually with family. I was excited for me, too; there was a dynamic that was not lost on me. I would get a chance to be alone with Clebe.

Someone had been around nearly every minute in the hospital. In the room, it was his roommate. Elsewhere, it was other patients or staff. Occasionally, we would find ourselves alone on an elevator when I was pushing him to dinner, but I longed for the opportunity to really have him to myself. Frankly, I didn't know what I'd do with him. He was still in very bad shape.

His stitches were infected and painful. He was still smarting over a recent operation that had employed a local anesthetic while the surgeon ferreted out metal fragments. His nose was still clogged with dried blood. His face was still swollen. And all his wounds had oozed over the new bandaging by the time we got to the car.

Still, I longed to hold him, to cuddle him, to press my body against his and tell him that I loved him just as much, as deeply, as completely. I wanted to assure him that he still appealed to me sexually, althought at this point we were unsure what the prognosis would be on that subject.

By the time we got to Dorsey and Lucille's house, Clebe was weak and pale. He leaned heavily on his daddy as Mr. McClary and I helped him out of the car, up the walk, and into the house. We weren't inside more than a few minutes, with Clebe sitting up in the living room, before he grew tired.

"I think I'd better lie down for a while."

Mr. Pat and I led him down the hall to a bedroom where we helped him stretch out on the bed. When the others left us, I quietly shut and locked the door. He was tired, anesthetized, uncomfortable, and in pain.

But he was mine and mine alone, if only to lie beside him as he slept.

CHAPTER 14

Sunshine

 turned toward the bed. Clebe appeared asleep already. My poor, sweet darling. He was virtually mummified. I tiptoed toward the bed, reminded of the times in the hospital when I'd longed to climb in beside him. There had been no room and no privacy.

Clebe looked like misery personified, his scarred and stitched face knitted with pain. His remaining arm was taped tightly to his side, and both legs were good for little but a few steps with lots of help. Even moving in bed was an excruciating ordeal, having to maneuver his tender, sore feet to get leverage. (If it hadn't been for my nurse's training, I wouldn't have noticed he was in danger of footdrop. His feet were curling downward until I notified a doctor who set up a foot board and gave him something to press against. He might never have walked again without that.)

Emotion flooded me as I slipped into bed beside him. I was in love. I was grateful. I pitied his fragile condition, but I was full of joy to be with him and to know he was alive. The odor was purulent, combining dead, rotting flesh, infection, and medicine. I even smelled the dull, tangy metallic odor of the shrapnel.

Clebe would never again be the youthful, healthy, whole Clebe McClary I had fallen in love with. But lying there next to him, considering the alternative, imagining him dying on a battlefield half a world away, I nearly wept. I rolled to my side facing him and touched his face gently in the few tiny spots where he wasn't scarred, stitched, or scabbed over. He opened his eye.

"I love you, Deanna."

I shushed him and studied him. His stump was heavily bandaged and stationary. Every other appendage seemed paralyzed or fragile. His nostrils were clogged with dried blood. He breathed noisily through his throat, as if snoring while awake. I kissed him gently, where I could. His lips were an impossibility, swollen twice their normal size and turned almost inside out.

I caressed his neck and shoulder and ran my fingers lightly down his arm, applying hardly any pressure to the bandages. I was overwhelmed with love. He had come back to me—not well, but alive. We would build from here. At first I fought the urge to wrap my arms around him, but I sensed he wanted me as close as I could get. I was cautious, hesitant, but I pressed myself tenderly against him. He was as thrilled as I was.

We had discussed the possibility that we might never make love again. No one knew what the prospects were. I told him that wasn't the main emphasis in my life. He joked that it was his. I assured him that if it developed that he was unable, I would accept it and love him all the more.

That day, in the quietness and privacy of that borrowed bedroom, in spite of all the obstacles, my shyness, his immobility, we sweetly and beautifully discovered the good news about the future of our physical relationship. It was as wonderful and loving as our honeymoon. With his being so necessarily passive, I had to put aside my normal modesty (almost prudishness) and play a different role. It wouldn't always be that way, but for that moment, that day, it was right and proper. Out of the deepest love I could imagine, I accepted my part and enjoyed it. It remains a precious, cherished memory.

I put out of my mind the dread fear that anything either of us did might aggravate a wound or push a piece of shrapnel to a life-threatening position. We loved each other fully, and then we talked quietly. We reminisced; we dreamed; we believed everything would be better. We decided not to look at the now, but to always look ahead.

Clebe's speech became slower. He was exhausted. His swollen eye began to blink more and more slowly. When he didn't respond to my next question, I fell silent. He slept soundly, breathing heavily in those horrible, throaty, rasping gasps. I pulled away from him and relaxed. He didn't stir. The afternoon sun intruded through the window, making the room warmer and twice as bright as when we'd entered. I eased out of bed and soundlessly pulled the shade. In the darkness I slipped back into bed and dozed.

Several minutes later I was jolted awake when his whole body jumped and he screamed.

"Help me! Dea! Mama! Help me!"

I panicked, grabbing my housecoat and reaching for the door. I feared he was having a heart attack. Just before I opened the door, he screamed again.

"Help me! I can't see!"

When I opened the door, light came from the hall—along with Mama and Daddy McClary—and calmed Clebe. He had dreamed of Vietnam, of Japan, of the air medivac transport, of an ambulance ride, of Bethesda, of getting out for an afternoon, of a difficult and painful ride to someone's home, of resting in a brightly lit room, of loving his wife, of dozing. But he'd had no recollection of my shutting the shade. He had awakened blind. For all he knew, it had all been a dream. Perhaps he was dead. It terrified him.

That was a harrowing, horrifying experience for me, too, and it served to make me even more compassionate toward him. I became alert to any signs that he was worrying about anything, a keen observer of even the slightest grimace.

In mid-July, Clebe was transferred to Philadelphia Naval Hospital, and a new chapter began in our lives. He would endure seven operations on his hand alone, thirty-three overall. The

Philadelphia facility specialized in prosthetics for multiple am-
putees, so where Clebe had been in the minority (almost a
novelty) at Bethesda, he was just a typical patient now.

Even that knowledge was therapeutic. At Bethesda, as
one of the most severely injured, you can start feeling really
sorry for yourself. That wasn't like Clebe, but both of us fell
into that trap because of the attention he got in Maryland. In
Philadelphia it was, "Join the club, soldier. What body parts
did you come back with?"

My last section of nurse's training had been in prosthetics, another divine coincidence. What I saw in Philadelphia, however, opened my eyes to a world I never knew
existed. The hospital was so huge and the population so vast
that it seemed everywhere you turned you saw shattered
bodies. I became all too familiar with the alphabet ramp, so
named because it led to all the wards, each designated with a
different letter. Over the next several months I would learn
that hospital, that ramp, and those wards. They imprinted
themselves so deeply on my mind that twenty years later I
could diagram them for you. And each area would evoke
powerful memories that reach my soul.

During the last few weeks at Bethesda and the first few at
Philadelphia, I developed a vocal cord problem that acted like
a tumor, which scared me to death. My left vocal cord became
thick, rigid, and nonfunctioning. Doctors diagnosed it as a
result of gross stress. I was hardly sleeping, going all day every
day, and talking with Clebe, the staff, other patients, anyone I
thought needed conversation. Before long I could hardly talk,
and there was no way I could sing.

Still, I tried to do my best. There were so many needy
men at Philadelphia, my heart went out to them. I brought
cookies and conversation to everyone who would give me the
time. When Clebe was in surgery, I couldn't stand the wait. I
needed something to do, so once I became familiar with the
staff on each floor of each ward and they recognized me, I was
free to make my own rounds. I moved from patient to patient,
trying to get each to talk.

Many were reluctant. Most severely wounded men were so horrified by their traumas that they didn't want to be reminded of how they were wounded, what had happened, how badly they had been hurt. Most told no one. Some went days without talking at all, assuming the doctors and nurses could see and know what was wrong, and thus they wouldn't have to discuss it. I even had to push and pull to get information out of Clebe; something told me that if I didn't get him to talk about it when it was freshest and most painful, it would set like concrete in his psyche and become another lifetime wound.

I started by asking a young man where he was from. If he looked offended or puzzled, I'd introduce myself and tell him who my husband was, that he was in surgery, and why. Then I probed gently.

"When were you wounded in Vietnam?"

"Where?"

"What happened?"

"How bad was it?"

More would talk than wouldn't, but those who wouldn't sometimes merely shuddered and trembled. That scared me, but I realized I was dealing with shell shock. They wouldn't talk about it, couldn't face it. Even today, as Clebe and I travel and speak and sing, Vietnam vets sometimes come out of their protective coverings to talk about what happened to them. Some haven't even told their closest loved ones in twenty years. When they begin to talk, they weep in great relief.

It seemed I was in that hospital twenty-four hours a day. The moment finally came when I was able to put Clebe's wounds, our problem, in proper perspective. I knew he wasn't unique. Many men were hurt worse than Clebe, but when I saw my first true basket case, I could feel only deep compassion for the victim and gratefulness for Clebe's fortune in comparison.

I had heard the term *basket case* but never knew what it meant. After greeting nearly everyone on both sides of a ward, passing out cookies and—I hope—encouragement and cheer, I noticed one more patient back in a corner. He lay on his back, unmoving. I stood staring at the armless, legless bust of a boy who couldn't have been twenty years old. And I wondered at the savagery of war. He was asleep, his cherubic, porcelain face peaceful and still. He breathed deeply through his nose, and I realized that his features were the only parts of his body the war had left unaffected.

I wanted to embrace him, to weep for him. I wondered about his family, his wife or girl friend, his friends. What could they say or do to relieve any of the agony? If he ever became completely free of pain, he would still be just a partial physical man: a brain, a digestive system, and a cardiovascular system. Would someone stimulate him with gentle massages every day? How else would he be aware of his world? What ingenious way would someone invent to help him communicate?

I've never been able to forget that image. It made me wonder why others left their loved ones when they found them in much less traumatized states. I wouldn't have wanted to see Clebe for the first time in a ward with twenty others, all looking on to see how the two of us would react to the sight of the other. More than once I noticed family groups of three or four huddled at the entrance to a ward, trying to see a loved one before he spotted them. Occasionally, a girl friend or even a wife would catch a glimpse of her man, burst into tears, and have to be led away. Nurses told me that most often such loved ones never returned, abandoning lovers disfigured beyond recognition.

Because it was a ward and not a single or double room, even the wounded who saw their families at the door wouldn't risk asking them to come in. The patients pretended not to see their loved ones until they had committed themselves to approach or slip away. That saved the embarrassment of the others knowing that your family came, refused to see you, and left you.

Admittedly, sometimes the wounded were so embittered that they drove their families away. Still, it was inconceivable to me how anyone could desert a man who had sacrificed his body for our country.

These were the men who called me Sunshine because I

always tried to bring them a smile. When no one else was around, when hardly anyone visited regularly, they could count on seeing me. Each was in a different stage of recovery, of course, and those who had learned to maneuver motorized wheelchairs began to enjoy life most quickly. In fact, they developed a certain comfort, a familiarity and acceptance of one another that allowed them to be raucous and mischievous. I learned that when many were released, they found no one who identified with them or understood them, and they became sullen, lonely, and almost eager to return to the familiar surroundings of the hospital.

Dealing with Clebe was not always idyllic. Though I was committed to being with him almost every waking minute, many days I'd have preferred sleeping in, especially when I had been with him until past midnight the night before. I was short-tempered because of that, and he was irritable simply out of the frustration of being so dependent. If my helping with his therapy hurt him, he might snap at me. I tried to keep sarcasm from my responses.

"I'm sorry, darlin', but I have to do this. It has to be done."

I became authoritative about getting him well, because I wanted him independent. When it was really frustrating for him and I couldn't appease him with a soft answer, I could be just as belligerent as he.

"Well, if you don't need me, maybe I should go back to Florence."

In truth, that was the last place I wanted to go, and he usually called my bluff.

"Well, go ahead then!"

That always got to me. But there was no way I was going to do that. We might fuss and nag, and there might be times when I wished I could just punch him, but I wasn't about to leave him. He was making me more independent than I wanted to be, and I was trying to do the same for him. Sure, there were times when I wanted to just be a housewife with a breadwinner who handled everything else. Clebe hated having to be waited on. The day would come when that would mostly end, but in the meantime, life was tough. And getting tougher.

The first time we got away from Philadelphia Naval Hospital for a few hours I carefully squeezed Clebe into our compact car and drove up into the mountains. He had just had a cast removed from his hand after yet another operation, and his hand looked pitiful. The only two functional fingers were stiff and straight, and the others were essentially useless.

It was rainy and cold, and that made all Clebe's aches and pains even worse. I enjoyed stopping at all the sights and shops and sales. As usual, I would strike up a conversation with anyone, including three college boys on their way back down the mountain after a Bible conference. They rhapsodized about the Bible and the Lord and what He had been doing in their lives and wasn't He wonderful and all that. We just chimed right in as if we knew what they were talking about. The fact is, we were nowhere spiritually, compared to them, but we didn't know it. In fact, I thought Clebe was one of the most devout and spiritual Christians I had ever met.

At an antique store I began chatting with some distinguished-looking men who said they were from Philadelphia.

"My husband's in the hospital there."

"Really? Where? We're physicians."

"At the Naval Hospital."

"That's where we practice."

A few minutes later I fell in love with an antique washstand and pleaded with Clebe to let it be our first furniture purchase since we'd been married. He reluctantly agreed, but I had no cash or credit cards and the merchant wouldn't take a check. One of the doctors from Philadelphia, however, recognized the problem.

"We'll cash your check, and you can pay the man."

We loaded that piece into the back of our car (it's still in our home two decades later), leaving just enough room for Clebe and me, and we headed back down the mountain. That encounter with the three Bible students and the touch of grace from the good doctors were harbingers we didn't recognize at the time.

In late July of 1968 Clebe's doctors advised that he go home for thirty days and build his strength before he attempted any more operations. All the surgery had taken a heavy toll. Clebe could walk some—very little—but he was weak and pale and thin. Everyone expected him to get better, and they knew that with the two of us working together, he would. But his progress had slowed because there is only so much any body can take.

Ma-Ma Willis sent us a clipping entitled "It All Depends on You," author unknown, that greatly encouraged Clebe:

> Take a slice of butter, a piece of meat, some sand, a brick, some clay, and pine shavings and put them on a fire. Each is subjected to the same agent, yet the butter melts, the meat fries, the sand dries, the clay hardens, and the shavings blaze.
>
> Just so, under identical influences, circumstances, and environment, one man becomes stronger, another weaker, and another withers. In the long run, what life does *to* you depends on what life finds *in* you.

On July 26, I drove Clebe all the way from Philadelphia to Florence, where we planned to stay with my parents for several of his thirty days of leave from the hospital. I was exhausted and sweaty, and the perfect flip hair style that was the rage at the time was only a flop for me. I was glad to get home and see everybody, but all I wanted to do was relax and get some of Mother's and Goggie's home cooking.

Poor Clebe. I should have known how eager he was to get out and do something. Even though the drive had been exhausting for him, too, he had been so confined in Philadelphia that he was heady with freedom. He had been allowed a few forays out, but his hand was fragile, his eye was precarious, and his fever often spiked, due to infection of his various wounds.

Once he was settled and comfortable in Florence, he was eager to pick up the local paper and catch up on the latest news.

"Hey, Dea! Bobby Richardson's gonna be out at the high school tonight. I believe I'd like to go."

"Who's that?"

"The former Yankee second baseman. He spoke to my team once. He's a real hero of mine."

"What's he doin' at the high school?"

"He and Vonda Kay Van Dyke are gonna be there with some evangelist—Billy Zeoli—for a crusade."

Vonda Kay Van Dyke? Now there was a name I knew! She had been Miss America in 1965. I figured Clebe knew, too, because there wasn't a red-blooded Marine anywhere who didn't want a peek at Miss America. Vonda Kay or not, I didn't want to go.

"Not tonight, Clebe. I look a mess, and I'm exhausted."

"I believe I'll go, honey. Why don't you come? We'd have to get goin' pretty soon."

"No way! Not the way I look! Remember, that's where you coached and I led cheers. That's just what the locals would love to see, me comin' back in all my glory with greasy, flopped hair, looking haggard. Forget it."

CHAPTER 15
Sonshine

I was in a mood. I had no interest in going to the crusade thing, whatever it was. In my mind, crusades were like revivals, and revivals were those things I saw on TV with women in floor-length black dresses and their hair up in buns. I didn't want to look like that, and I didn't want to sing like that. To me, that was the Dark Ages.

Most of all, I didn't want to make my triumphal return to my high-school football stadium looking like I did, after having been Miss Florence, after being one of the first to have a big wedding and sendoff, and after having been the wife of one of the most famous Vietnam veterans in the state of South Carolina. The news of Clebe's wounds and the progress of his recovery had been in all the papers, so I knew the first time we appeared in public in our hometown, we would be scrutinized. I wasn't ready for that.

"Deanna, honey, I need you to drive me out there."

"Clebe, I am not going. Do you understand? I am in no mood or condition to go, and you aren't either. Why do you want to go to that? We just got home."

"I'm goin' to go, Dea. If you don't wanna go, maybe your mother will take me."

Mother would have done anything for Clebe. "Sure, I'll take you. We'd best be going soon, Dea."

"Y'all can go without me."

I went to a back bedroom to fuss and pout, and I slammed the door to make my point. I heard them all getting ready and heading out to the car, and I hoped somebody, anybody, might stay with me. I heard someone talking his way through helping Clebe to the car.

"Easy. Steady. I've got you. Okay."

Car doors slammed. And Mother knocked on my door. She was clearly mad. "Deanna, I wish you would take a look at yourself in the mirror."

I didn't respond. I didn't like looking in the mirror. I didn't like the person I saw.

"Look in the mirror, young lady, and think how God has blessed you. You're worried about your friends seeing you when you're not at your best, and there goes Clebe with his face shot off. How do you think that makes him feel?"

It hurt that she talked so mean to me. I glowered at her. She wouldn't back down. "Well, you just stay here then. You'll be here in this house by yourself, because we're all going."

Someone honked the horn. I pressed my lips tight and breathed angrily through my nose. I didn't want to stay home alone. I was being shamed into going, but I wasn't going to accept it easily. I certainly wasn't going to like it. When Mother turned on her heel and hurried out, I grabbed my purse and followed her.

I was the last one in the car, and someone said something about my making them late. I said nothing, just slammed the door, looked straight ahead, and fumed the whole way. There was no turning back now. I would be humiliated as soon as anyone recognized me.

I was stunned to see how packed the stands were when we got there.

"Oh, Clebe, let's not go in. There won't be any place to sit. C'mon, Clebe. Please."

He had learned to ignore me. He hobbled slowly ahead, into the stadium, looking up and down the rows of seats. The only ones open were in the back, which required climbing the stadium steps all the way up. Without hesitating, Clebe began working his way up. I felt as if every eye in the stadium were on us. I was mortified, trying to hide.

I whispered, "Clebe!"

He kept moving. I knew it was my tantrum that had made us late and now had forced him to show his independence. Someone tried to help him, but he wouldn't be helped in public. He slowly and painstakingly made his way up to the last available row of seats. All I could do was follow. I worried about my hair, my makeup, my outfit, and simply looking nutty going to a crusade. I believed in God. Clebe read the Bible for us every night and prayed before every meal, so I knew he didn't need this. I was embarrassed, never once stopping to think that anyone who saw me would also be a nut at an evangelistic crusade. Besides that, who would look at a woman when there was a mummified serviceman with one arm and one eye struggling along?

All my thoughts were on me, believing I would be compared to Miss America while I looked like a hag. Comparing, comparing, comparing, feeling sorry for myself, sick of myself, a sorry package.

Soon after we settled in, Bobby Richardson spoke. I was still pouting and refused to listen to a word he said. Clebe was all ears, and that made me all the madder. I was not going to cooperate.

Then it was Vonda Kay's turn. She sang and performed as a ventriloquist. I checked her out and, in the process, missed her message entirely. Unfortunately for me, a petty, self-centered, comparing former beauty queen, Vonda Kay sang beautifully, was very talented, and looked wonderful. I was jealous, but at least she had gotten my attention. I became a little more receptive and realized this wasn't a show from the Dark Ages after all. It was impressive.

When Billy Zeoli began to speak, I was captivated. He was stylish and sharp. He was enthusiastic and exuded charisma. He told stories, dramatized them, was funny, convincing, exciting, dynamic. He exhibited the most profound faith, talking about Jesus Christ as if Jesus were his best friend. I half expected Jesus to be the next speaker, that's how familiar Billy made Him sound.

Billy spoke with such conviction that I was intrigued. He spoke of Noah, a man who lived in the desert and had never seen a drop of rain, building an ark to protect his family against a flood the Lord had told him about. Noah's friends said he was crazy, a fool. What is rain? they said. Billy said Noah had indeed been a fool, a fool for God.

"He heard the voice of God. He obeyed the voice of God. And he was victorious. He was a fool for God. Whose fool are you?"

Then Billy spoke of General Joshua who announced the battle plan and led his men around the walls of Jericho thirteen times in seven days. He was surely ridiculed as a fool until those walls fell down, just as God had told him.

"Joshua heard the voice of God. He obeyed the voice of God. And he was victorious. He was a fool for God. There are only two kinds of fools in this world. A fool for Christ and a fool for others. Whose fool are you?"

I didn't want to answer that question. I didn't want to be anybody's fool. But I knew I wasn't a fool for God. Billy kept preaching.

"There are only three things you can say to Jesus Christ: yes, no, or maybe. If you say yes, you're saying, 'Lord Jesus, I know that You came to live a perfect example for me, that bearing all my sins You died on that cross. You were buried and rose again from the dead so I could have eternal life in You. I believe in You and trust You and thank You for the forgiveness of my sins. Thank You for the new and abundant life You promise. [Boy, did I need *that*!]'

"If you say yes, you can know where you're going to spend eternity, even if you died right now."

Billy Zeoli's speaking of death was hitting close to home. I had been close to death and dying in those hospitals. Clebe was a walking time bomb and had frequently been closer to death than to life. Though I had believed in the Lord all my life, I had never settled the question of Jesus as my Savior; I had never honestly dealt with where I would spend eternity.

Billy explained that saying no would bring its own results; that a person who says no would be Satan's fool, guaranteed of eternity in hell without God. I wasn't concerned with a negative answer. That wasn't an option for me. I would never say no to God. I believed in God, but I had no guarantee of heaven. I might say maybe, but never no.

Billy Zeoli was reading my mind.

"The maybe category is a very dangerous place. It carries with it an X factor: the death factor. When you die, your maybe becomes an automatic no in the eyes of God if you've never said yes to the Lord Jesus."

My heart was pounding. I *was* a "maybe." Billy began snapping his fingers in front of the microphone in the cadence of a heartbeat. My heart beat in sync with his snaps.

"At any second (snap, snap, snap), you may die (snap, snap, snap). You're one heartbeat (snap, snap) from hell (snap)."

I knew it was true. I had never said yes to Jesus, had never asked Him to forgive my sins, to come into my life, to save my soul. I had never realized that need. I knew I was a sinner, and now I knew a way to be forgiven and cleansed. It sounded so wonderful. I knew where I stood and where I wanted to stand, as Billy invited people to receive Christ.

"All over this place I want you to bow your heads and close your eyes. If you mean business with the Lord tonight, if you want to receive Him as your Savior, get that void filled and things settled in your life, I want you to very quietly raise your hand. No one is looking. It's just between you and God. Say yes to the Lord Jesus right now."

I wanted to raise my hand. I wanted to say yes. A battle raged in my mind.

I didn't even want to be here. I can't do this. I can't respond. This is the most foolish thing I could possibly do. I know the Lord. Why am I feeling this way? It's just emotional, just a feeling. I'm just feeling bad about myself now because I'm not perfect. But I'm human. Who is perfect? Anyway, why do I have to raise my hand?

*I'm close enough to heaven on these bleachers that God has to
know my decision.*

Billy persisted.

"Whose fool are you? God's fool? Someone else's fool?
Satan's fool? Your own fool? The biggest fool in this place is
the person who will sit here right now and hear God's simple
plan of salvation then walk away saying no or maybe."

That was me! I wanted Jesus. I wanted to say yes. But
first I raised my eyes and peeked around. I knew it was a very
personal, private decision, and that's the way I wanted it. I
didn't want anyone else to see or know. The other people
seemed to have their heads bowed and eyes closed. I closed
mine again, too, and slipped my hand up and down quickly,
my bangle bracelets making an embarrassing racket. My little
sister told me later that hearing that sound gave her the courage to raise her hand, too.

Billy then challenged those of us who had raised our
hands to take a stand and acknowledge the Lord publicly in
front of our friends and families.

"How serious are you?"

I was serious, but this was too much. I was up there in the
bleachers, closer to heaven than most anyone else. The Lord
had seen my hand. He knew my heart. I couldn't walk forward. The battle continued to rage.

A part of me wanted to run down there, to say yes to
Jesus. I *was* desperate to get my life straightened out. But I
didn't want to look like a fool. And there was that word again.
Whose fool *was* I? Billy seemed to know my heart again.

"If you can walk away and reject God tonight, you *are* the
biggest fool." I decided to take the first step. My leg never
weighed so much. I stepped out. I was oblivious of Clebe and
my family and anyone else who cared to see who was walking
down those steps. What a sense of relief, of knowing I was
doing the right thing!

I became aware of steps behind me. People flocked toward the platform. I had worried that my friends would think
I needed help. Well, I *did* need help! I glanced behind me, and

who should be coming but Clebe! How sweet! He would support me. The way I had treated him that evening, he probably wanted to make sure I got there. People passed me as I waited for him to negotiate the stairs one by one. He could barely bend one knee; the other was stiff and straight.

I had hoped he would come down with me. I needed him with me. I wanted Jesus and I wanted heaven, but frankly, most of all, I wanted to become what I thought Clebe was. If walking down there in public was the price of becoming a person like Clebe, it was worth it. I was drawn by the message, convicted by the Holy Spirit, and inspired by Clebe.

"Clebe, thank you so much for coming down with me."

"Honey, I'm not comin' down for you; I'm comin' down for me."

If I'd had false teeth, they'd have hit the ground. If there was one person in the world I thought already knew the Lord personally, it was my husband. I wondered if he had said what he said just to have a reason to help me get there. When we arrived in the infield, several counselors thanked us for coming forward and being good examples, but Clebe finally pulled aside Sam Anderson, a pastor, and asked him to pray with us for salvation. When I heard Clebe ask Christ to be his Savior, I knew I had been mistaken about him. He had been a good man, but he had not truly been a Christian. How wonderful to become Christians the same evening!

Afterward we attended a social where several prominent Christians congratulated us. For the life of me, I couldn't understand what *we* had done that was so special. God had saved us. We had gratefully received Christ, and we were overwhelmed. Clebe was asked to share his testimony the next night. He agreed, but he didn't even know what a testimony was. We now know that he should have declined that invitation and grown in the Lord before trying to minister publicly, and that's what we recommend for new believers. As our dear friend Harold Morris advises in his book *Twice Pardoned,* "preparation before performance."

I was also asked to speak at a crusade the next month, just

before Clebe. I was so scared I admitted that I was kicking off my shoes so my knees wouldn't shake so much. I was uncomfortable and I didn't want to speak, but I felt I needed to. I told of all the years I thought I had been a Christian, identifying myself as one because I claimed my grandmother's faith.

"But faith cannot be inherited. It must be received and exercised personally."

I also talked about my father's being an alcoholic. I knew he had claimed faith in Christ when he was a young Marine, overseas in Japan, and he had been a Sunday school superintendent for several years. Now I asked people to pray that I would have genuine love and forgiveness in my heart for him and that he would be drawn back to the Savior.

"That night, July 26, 1968, I met Jesus Christ as my Savior. I also realized He wanted to be the Lord of every area of my life that was destroying me. In a very short while I learned what God's transforming power was all about. The same sun that hardens clay is the same sun that melts wax, that melts butter. Jesus Christ came into my sin-hardened heart, filled with bitterness and hatred, melted and molded it and gave me the ability to love for the first time in my life.

"As Jesus Christ loves us sinners so much that He was willing to die on the cross for our sins, suddenly I was able to look at my daddy, unchanged in any way, and love him. At this point I was able to pray for my daddy. I was able to look at him, eyeball to eyeball, and really talk to him.

"'Daddy, I just want you to know the peace and joy I've found in Jesus Christ, the forgiveness and the true love.'

"I didn't know if he would curse me or slap me or ridicule me, but tears welled up in his eyes. I knew then that God was going to work in my daddy's life and restore him. Second Corinthians 5:17 tells us that when a man is in Christ, he is a new creature. Old things pass away and all things become new."

I had no idea how effective or ineffective my efforts were until afterward when a new convert—an alcoholic himself—told counselors that something I had said about my father had gotten through to him. That's when I knew that God could use me, if I was willing. I prayed and prayed that He would restore my voice so I could sing, but I was impressed that He would not allow that until I was willing to use my voice to speak for Him. That would take awhile because I was an unwilling speaker.

I promised the Lord that I would sing only for Him and also that I would love a simple assignment like dressing Clebe, feeding Clebe, bathing Clebe, doing anything for Clebe. I'd have him wherever he needed to be on time, whatever it took.

"Lord, just let me be the helpmate. That's where I'm happiest. That's all I want to be."

I was asked to sub for Clebe when he was unable to speak at a small church near Florence. I was nervous and would have loved to get out of it, but even Daddy encouraged me to do it. He and Mother went with me. It was the first time they heard my testimony, and I gave it pretty much as I've presented it here. I didn't know if it would hurt or offend Daddy; I just knew I had to say it all.

I was honest about the fact that I had hated my daddy and that I even prayed that he would die. I felt led to give an invitation, asking people to reconcile with their families. The renewal, the rededications, and the reunifying of homes were moving and awesome to me. I asked my parents to come down and pray with me, and Daddy just cried and cried.

From the point of my conversion, I started praying for him rather than hating him. He didn't quit drinking right away, but the bad episodes became fewer and farther between. I prayed for seven years that he would be victorious over alcohol and return to his first love of Christ. I had to be taught faith and God's faithfulness.

Thirteen years ago Daddy finally gave up alcohol for good. My prayers were answered. I'm now proud to say he's my father. When his old friends ask about him, I tell them, "You should see him now. He's a new man."

It's true. Dean Fowler, Sr., is an example to me. He's living proof of what true forgiveness can do for a person.

Clebe and I spent much of the rest of that all-too-short thirty-day leave on the beach. The Lord used the familiar surroundings, the heat, the sun, and the saltwater to quickly heal Clebe. Facial scars began to fade, and the leg that had appeared like ground beef was healing beautifully. Slowly, Clebe began to build himself back up to his firm, muscular physique. Two years of deliberate and frustrating rehabilitation lay ahead in Philadelphia for Clebe, yet slowly and surely, he began to mend.

During his first few weeks at Philadelphia Naval Hospital, I had stayed with Frank and Elaine Hayes, friends of the McClarys. Elaine kept me active, teaching me how to sew and taking me to antique stores, which was great therapy for me. Now that he was going to be a patient during the week and an outpatient on weekends, we rented our second apartment, in Barrington, New Jersey. What a treat to have our own little home again! We hadn't had a place to ourselves since Quantico. Clebe's Daddy had built us a home on his farm while Clebe was overseas, but it would be some time before we could move in there.

I enjoyed fixing up our New Jersey apartment, and I was pleased that Clebe was ambulatory—though his hand was useless for months. I still had to do almost everything for him; he was in constant pain and tired easily.

By early 1969, I was pregnant. I couldn't slow down in caring for Clebe because we were now racing for him to be more independent before I got to the point that *I* needed to be looked after. I turned up the throttle on his rehabilitation; I didn't do anything for him I thought he could do for himself. I left him in the rain, fumbling with the car door, instead of opening it for him. It was time he learned to work at it.

"Do you expect me to open doors for you? You're the man. You're supposed to be the chivalrous one."

I'm sure it frustrated him and made him mad, but today he thanks me for it.

Another time, during dinner at the hospital, relatives

were visiting and looking daggers at me because I wouldn't assist him in trying to shovel peas in his mouth. I had laced a fork to his fingers, but he wasn't doing well. It was awkward, yet I refused to let anyone help him, and he caught on soon enough.

During those days, I began to learn how to relate to the new Clebe. I caught his moods by the look on his face, or when he was a little short with me. At first I took such moods and responses personally. I'd wonder what I did wrong, how I had failed. I felt like a wounded puppy. Either I became reactive or I felt sorry for myself, wondering why he couldn't see what I was doing for him. Eventually, I realized that we had to go through such times as a couple. These were the hard parts, the rough areas, learning each other's reactions.

I know many wives get mad when their husbands don't communicate, but I learned that sometimes he won't tell me things because he can't. It's then my job to find ways to communicate, to read him, to understand him intuitively. I don't want to force him into my mold, to make him as verbal as I am. It wouldn't be any good either if I was just like him.

I wanted to do whatever it took to bring him back to full health, and so I needed to know what he needed, even if he wouldn't or couldn't tell me. I noticed that he was most irritable when he was in pain, and pain was one thing he would never complain about. I had my clue. I could tell when he was hurting because it made him irritable, but his irritability hurt me. I had to learn to not take it personally, but consider it his way of communicating, so I could help rather than make the situation worse.

If he was short with me, rather than shoot back with a short remark or act hurt, I would back off being pushy about anything, let him rest, help him get a bath, whatever would make him feel better. He always seemed chipper in the morning after breakfast, so I tried to plan around that, too. I raised important issues when I knew he was feeling better and in a mood to talk. Sure, I would have preferred to live on my timetable, but as I learned his and was able to accept it, we were both happier.

One weekend at our apartment I complained I wasn't feeling well. Clebe tried to talk me out of it, telling me the discomfort was in my head. I resented that after all I had done for him, but I knew he was desperate—as I was—not to have me out of commission.

I don't believe Clebe intended to be insensitive. He was fragile, exhausted, in constant pain. He could walk short distances, but he had to rest frequently. And I had to help him do almost everything that required hands or fingers.

"Honey, just take some aspirin and come to bed."

"Clebe, it feels like a knife stabbing my bladder, and I'm passing pure blood."

"Dea, I just got out of the hospital, and I'll be due back there soon enough. Please, let's don't go to a hospital."

I passed more blood and my temperature was rising. I knew something was wrong. I had to get to a doctor.

"Clebe! All I need is to be seen by a doctor so he can prescribe something. Then I'll be okay. You can wait in the car, but I don't want to go alone."

CHAPTER *16*

A New Invalid

$\mathcal{I}$ could have been to a doctor and back in the time it took to help Clebe into the car, but I felt a lot better driving when he was with me. If I passed out, he could at least get help. He waited in the car while I saw a urologist in the emergency room. The tests took a long time, and I worried about Clebe's patience. Finally the doctor returned, looking concerned.

"I'm sorry, Mrs. McClary, but I can't let you go home in your condition. You need to spend the night here."

"What? I've had this condition before. I'll live with it. Just give me something for it."

"Ma'am, this is bordering on nephritis—more serious than what you've had all your life. Your temperature is near 105. If your kidneys shut down, which it appears they might, you could suffer toxemia, which would threaten your baby."

Now he had gotten my attention.

"Can I at least go home and get my robe?"

"No. We have gowns here."

"But my husband is a wounded veteran, barely ambulatory. He needs constant help, and there's no one else."

"He can stay in the same room with you, ma'am. I'll order a cot or an extra bed."

"Oh, thank you!"

By that time Clebe's impatience and curiosity brought him hobbling into the hospital. After stopping at the front desk, he limped into the emergency room, looking much worse than anyone else there.

"Clebe, they're admitting me."

"I heard."

"The doctor is arranging a cot or a bed for you, whichever you want."

"No, Deanna. I'm not stayin' in this hospital a single night."

"Clebe, you've got to! I'm scared! I don't want to stay here alone!"

"Dea, I can't stand it. I can't stand any of it. I've had all I can take of hospitals, and I've got to get away from here."

I begged him to stay, grilling him on how he thought he was going to get home, not being able to drive or even to walk far. I was scared about my illness and the future of my pregnancy. I thought he had flipped out, thinking he could even unlock the front door without help. His hand was virtually useless, and he had a big spacer ball in his eye that had to come out every night.

"How are you going to get home?"

"Someone will give me a ride."

I could understand that Clebe was sick of the hospital, but I couldn't understand why he wouldn't stay with me one night. He told me he loved me, which I found hard to believe just then, and I wept as he walked away. I rolled to my side and parted the blinds so I could see him as he walked across the grounds to the dimly lit corner.

His hand was in a huge bandage, so he couldn't even stick his thumb out for a ride. He just stood at that corner, frail and pathetic in the night, waving at cars as they drove by. People must have thought he was an escapee. Finally a late model car stopped, and Clebe leaned in the window to talk to the driver. I assumed it was a doctor, and I was right. Clebe told me later the doctor had driven him home and unlocked the front door for him.

I was scared I was going to die. I felt like a POW, confined, controlled, imprisoned. I was being fed intravenously and was also drinking as much water as I could hold to force my kidneys to work. But I couldn't get anyone to bring me a bedpan, so I was in severe pain. Still, I called some neighbors and told them to watch out for Clebe. By the time they got to the apartment, the front door was unlocked, and they walked right in. They found Clebe on the bed, fully dressed, shoes still on, arm up, one leg stiff, his good eye shut in a deep sleep, his spacer eye staring lifelessly at the world. He was a sight.

They woke him to feed him, and he had them dial our mothers so mine could stay in the hospital with me the next day and his could take care of him. During that time, while Clebe's mother was helping him in the bathroom, he broke down and sobbed.

"I can't believe Dea has to do all this stuff for me, and she never complains!"

His mother tried to comfort him.

"Well, honey, she loves you. And so do I. You don't need to worry about me. I changed your diapers when you were a baby, so this is no big deal to me."

Clebe realized how much he needed me and began to feel guilty about having left me in the hospital alone overnight. He was sweet when he visited. His mother, however, was wrong when she thought taking care of him would be no big deal. It wasn't in the sense that it didn't sicken her, but with all the lifting and stretching and pulling she had to do that weekend, she cracked a couple of ribs.

Clebe's and my relationship was a little different for a while after that. Clebe moved toward more sensitivity, and of course, both of us wanted our child to be healthy and to have a mother who would be up to taking care of both a baby and a husband who still needed help. I was soon back doing whatever I could for Clebe, which included a lot of explaining to curious strangers about what had happened to him.

It bothered Clebe when people stared, and I usually noticed, too. I would walk right up to people and ask them if they wanted to know how he lost his arm and his eye. I told them of his sacrifice for our country. Children who stared or said anything were often yanked away by embarrassed parents, but children were so innocent and honest that I enjoyed talking with them the most.

The time came, as I should have known it would, when Clebe grew tired of my living my life through him. I had no life of my own. It seemed I was clinging to him like a leech. I was comfortable in that role. I thought I was making him independent, but I was really robbing him of his freedom to grow. That's when he started telling me I had to find myself again, to develop my own interests and things I liked to do.

"You can't be me."

That cut me deeply. I admired Clebe, and I *wanted* to be a part of him.

"I am you. I'm as much you as anybody I know. I want to be like you, think like you, act like you."

But Clebe wouldn't have it. He had taken marriage and family courses in college and would lecture me on the fact that a couple needs both time together and time apart.

"You've got your own life, too. You can't just live your partner's life. You're givin' yourself to me totally, and it's makin' you less of a person. I 'preciate what you're tryin' to do, but you've got a whole lot to offer and you need to be out doin' other things, too. You need to be by yourself some."

Clebe finally admitted that he felt he would heal better if I gave him some room every day. He had wearied of entertaining all the visitors who had come hundreds of miles to see him in the hospital. He was grateful for and even overwhelmed by their concern, but entertaining them while trying to recuperate set him back. So we began to decline some of the offers to visit and I began to give Clebe the room he needed to rest.

Although Clebe would be in and out of the hospital over a two-and-a-half-year period following the attack that nearly took his life, he was discharged from the Marine Corps in July of 1969, months before our first child was born. We finally moved to the home his daddy had built for us on two acres of his five-hundred-acre farm. I should have been in heaven, but I wasn't.

Clebe accepted a position as a probation and parole officer for the state of South Carolina. Some people thought that his getting the job was a wonderful break, a great deal for a wounded veteran. I think at first even Clebe thought so. His dream had been to get into coaching, but there wasn't much demand for a one-armed, one-eyed coach. (I believe he could have, and still could, become a fantastic coach. He wouldn't admit it, but I'm sure he knows it, too.)

Many thought Clebe would be a wonderful example to troubled offenders. And I'm sure he was. More than two hundred parolees of all ages reported to him every month, and his job was to try to get them jobs and to keep them gainfully employed and out of jail. In those few cases in which he was successful, he feels a great deal of justifiable pride. Most of the offenders, however, committed more crimes within a few months.

Clebe is the type who likes to finish what he starts, but he soon grew tired of trying to counsel and help people who were seeing him only because they were forced to, people who were ungrateful, and people who had no idea what he was talking about when he encouraged good manners, hard work, honesty, loyalty, and all that had made him the man he was.

I hated that job from the day he took it. He got to know all those parolees and their families and friends, and they would call him in the middle of the night, wanting him to come and talk them out of committing suicide and who knows what else. Life was not what I had expected. To me, there was a terrible enemy, waiting outside our home, an enemy that was out to get us. It seemed as if our whole world was suddenly wicked.

I was very pregnant by that time, and quite angry. I felt rejected whenever Clebe left me to work with someone. I pleaded, begged, and cajoled to get him to stay home, but he was a man of duty and honor. He didn't argue with me. He just went out and did what he had to do.

There were times I despised him for that. He made me so mad! I thought he was the most insensitive man I'd ever met. Yet if he had given in and catered to my selfish childishness, I would have wound up not respecting him today. I had to come to grips with the fact that he would not be run by his wife, that he would do what he thought was right, no matter what I thought. Some of the time, I was right. That didn't matter. I tried to reason with him. It didn't work.

I was terrified to be alone, especially when anonymous callers breathed heavily into the phone or used obscene language. Clebe advised me to quote Scripture to them. If you've never tried it, believe me, it works. The next time I answered a call and heard that heavy breathing and the beginnings of an obscene remark, I simply shut my eyes and began quoting John 3:16: "For God so loved the world that He gave . . ."

Click.

Some of the farming was also our responsibility, so when after a hard day we were awakened in the middle of the night by escaped cows grazing in our front yard, I had to get up, help dress Clebe, and send him out to round them up. My dream of a blissful married life in our first house was still just a dream.

When I felt up to it, I traveled with Clebe. In August, two months before our first child was due, I went with him to a crusade in Kannapolis, North Carolina. He was to speak Saturday night, but we went up a day early to see Billy Zeoli and Bobby Richardson and other friends and to see how the crusade went the first night. After the meeting we went to a social, then caught a ride back to our hotel with Lee and Betty Fisher—a wonderful couple then with Teen Crusades.

Lee pulled out of a small subdivision and started across the Concord-Kannapolis Highway. I had a strange feeling that we should hurry, but I said nothing. The next instant we were smashed from the left, a police car ramming my door, spinning us three times, nearly throwing us into oncoming traffic. The sound of tires burning on the pavement and the sickening crunch of the metal is with me to this day. All the windows were smashed and went flying, and all four doors were wedged shut.

The door had driven my Bible into my left hip, and the Bible acted as a fulcrum to my leg, which splayed out crazily from the dislocated ball and socket. My body felt hot, as if I were burning, and I realized I was fighting to stay alive. The four of us were stunned to silence at first, and I kept telling myself it was a bad dream, a nightmare. I wanted to wake up.

I didn't want to die. I fought it, then I wondered why I was fighting. I turned to look at Clebe.

"Are you okay, Clebe? Are you okay? I can't move, Clebe. I'm paralyzed."

My mind whirled. I couldn't think straight. Lee hung out the window, unconscious. Betty called to him several times, then realized no one was coming to help. She tried her door.

"We have to get out of here!"

She climbed through the window as people began to gather. I slipped in and out of consciousness as a tranquillity swept over me. I told myself to relax, that I had nothing to worry about. Liquid poured onto the pavement as people stood around with cigarettes. Until that moment Betty had been fairly controlled. Suddenly soft-spoken, mild-mannered Betty panicked and screamed at them: "Put those out! Can't you see there's gasoline all over! Someone help us!"

Dazed, I noticed Clebe struggling to get out. Someone pulled Lee out. Then Clebe. Someone else approached me. After trying the door, he leaned in the window and checked to see how I was. He noticed my leg in a bizarre position.

"We can't bring her out through the window. We'll have to get that door off. I think she's pregnant."

I heard women in the crowd gasp and repeat the word.

"Pregnant. She's pregnant."

I wondered who they were talking about and hoped against hope we hadn't hit a pregnant woman.

Not a baby! Please, not a poor little baby!

And I was out again. The cool night air hit me as my stretcher was shoved into the ambulance, and I realized how close my head was to the ceiling.

Oh, no! I forgot! I'm wearing that hair piece I lied about!

Clebe, who hates fake hair pieces, had complimented me on my hair that night.

"It *is* yours, isn't it?"

"Of course, honey. You know I wouldn't wear a hair piece, knowing how you feel about them."

A bald-faced lie, no question. I was scared to death—even before I realized *I* was the pregnant woman they were worried about—that something would catch my hair piece, tear it off, and expose me to my husband.

The nightmare suddenly became vivid again. More screeching tires! People screaming! Ambulance attendants leaping to safety! A huge car, headlights careening, sliding right toward the ambulance. I lay there helpless. The automobile stopped within inches. The driver of a stolen Cadillac had happened upon the scene and assumed he was facing a roadblock. He was going to blast through but realized he was heading for an ambulance at the last instant. Just in time.

I drifted off again, my heart slamming against my rib cage. When I came to, I was in the hospital. I felt dizzy, as if surrounded by a mist from a TV melodrama. My stretcher was being run down the hall by two doctors and two nurses who rammed it through sets of swinging double doors. I caught a glimpse of Clebe and Bobby and Betsy Richardson, who had just arrived. Betsy is such a saint. I was grateful she was there. I've never been with Betsy when I didn't feel as if I'd been on a mountaintop with the Lord, and I know it's because that's where she resides.

"Bobby, please pray for us! Pray for Lee! Pray for Betty! Pray for me!"

I was being rushed to have x-rays taken so the doctors would know what to do with my strange dislocation and see how the baby was doing. Every time I passed faces I recognized I pleaded with them to pray for us. I heard Lee had been admitted to intensive care. That worried me.

"Clebe, Betsy! Pray for Lee! Pray for us, please!"

Clebe had heard enough. He said something to me he had never said before and hasn't said since.

"Honey, would you shut up? Everybody *is* praying for us. You sound like a Holy Roller preacher!"

I pleaded with Betsy to go into x-ray with me, and it's a good thing I did. The girl there tried to force my leg flat so she could get a proper exposure, but the pain was unbearable. Betsy held my face in her hands and spoke softly to me, trying to comfort me and tell me everything was going to be all right. I screamed. Betsy turned toward the girl.

"Please don't do that to her."

"I have to get the leg flat."

"Well, honey, it won't go flat. Don't you see? That's what's wrong with it. You could injure her worse or harm her baby."

The girl still had my leg in her hands when the doctor walked in.

"What are you doing? Get away from her! That hip is clearly dislocated, and you can do more harm than good. You could cripple her for life!"

CHAPTER *17*

Saving the Baby

*T*he doctor dismissed the x-ray girl and brought in someone else to work the equipment. The ordeal was excruciating, but I knew it was necessary. The x-ray negative was shot with my leg in its crazy, dislocated position.

The doctor told me he was going to try to manipulate my leg to see if he could pop it back into place.

"Let me give you something for the pain first."

I knew better than that. "No, sir! I don't want it because of the baby. I can do it. I'm tough. I can stand the pain. Do what you have to do, but don't give me any medication."

He pursed his lips and shook his head, then started the manipulation without painkillers.

I screamed, "Betsy, I don't think I can stand this! Stop! I *can't* stand it!"

The doctor stopped and asked someone to call an orthopedic specialist.

"Let him see the x-rays, if they're finished."

A few minutes later the specialist—Dr. Curlee—hurried in, angry with the original doctor.

"You've not tried to manipulate yet, have you?"

"Well, yes, I thought I could . . ."

"Have you seen the x-rays?"

"No, they weren't ready, and . . ."

"You were manipulating without reading the films?"

"Well, I . . ."

"This is a very abnormal dislocation, Doctor. How did this happen?"

"Auto accident."

"Makes sense. There's a 65-degree-angled, pie-shaped wedge gouged out at the head of the femur."

The first doctor left, and Dr. Curlee spoke to me alone.

"Mrs. McClary, I understand that you don't want any medication that might harm your baby, but I want you to trust me that we will handle everything. We need to put you to sleep to attempt a closed reduction. Do you know what that is?"

"Yes, sir. I think I do."

"Okay, so even though we hope we don't have to go in and put a pin in there, you will need to be asleep for this procedure."

"Oh, please, doctor, don't put me to sleep."

He was soft-spoken and reassuring. "We'll take care of everything. We have to do this."

I felt the encouraging pressure of Betsy Richardson's hands on my shoulders. I sighed.

"Okay. If it has to be, it has to be."

As I was being prepped for the operation, I was reminded of my hair piece. Suddenly, that became my top priority again. I whispered desperately to the nurse.

"My husband doesn't like hair pieces, and he doesn't know I have one on. Could you just throw this in the trash? I never want to see it again. I lied to my husband, and I feel just awful."

But here came Clebe. In one motion, she swept that hair piece off my head, tucked it into her dress, and walked out right past him.

The closed reduction was a success, but Dr. Curlee had a problem. Normally, he said, he would have stabilized the leg with a body cast from the hip down. With me so pregnant, he was unable to stabilize the leg at all. I would be flat on my back for the next two months before the baby arrived.

When I regained consciousness in the recovery room, Dr.

Curlee stood over me. I looked directly into his eyes and told him I thanked the Lord for him and loved him. A specialist who operated on someone almost every day, he was surprised and delighted. He hadn't seen someone so immediately lucid after surgery.

"And no patient has ever said anything that nice to me."

I was in intensive care that night when my parents arrived. Though the nurses monitored the baby's progress all night, I was too frightened to sleep. I must have dozed just before morning. When I awoke at dawn, my stomach was hard as a brick, and I was suffering terrible pain. I moaned and the nurses came running.

Within a few seconds they flew me down the hall, IVs trailing, and prepped me for the labor room. I was in such a twilight zone that I hadn't even associated the hardness of my stomach and the pains with early labor. This was much, much too early. I was terrified.

An older ob-gyn, Dr. Wilson, approached me calmly.

"Mrs. McClary, you must relax. If you can help us out by staying calm, we're going to do everything we can to save your baby's life. You've been through quite a trauma, and I can make no guarantees, but we're going to do our best to stop this premature labor and let you carry this baby to term."

Mother cried, and normally, I would have been devastated and gone to pieces. But I knew panicking would be the worst thing for my baby. God gave me grace and His special peace that passes all understanding. We were surprised I was able to get pregnant in the first place, after all of Clebe's injuries. I believed God had given us this child, and though it was His right to take it if He saw fit, I didn't think He would.

I may not have been as relaxed as Dr. Wilson would have preferred, but I was at peace. Until his next comment.

"We're going to give you alcohol intravenously to reduce the contractions."

I almost wanted to jump off that bed and run. I was more frightened of the alcohol than anything.

"Please don't do that! I don't want any alcohol! My

daddy's had a problem with alcohol, and I don't want to act crazy. I want to be aware of what I'm saying and doing."

"It's not going to affect you that way, Mrs. McClary. We have to do it. The longer you carry this baby, the better it will be for both of you."

That got my attention, but I was still wary, scared I would act like a violent drunk. Those who were there that morning say I forced my eyes to stay open wide so I could remain aware of everything around me. As labor continued and pain increased, I refused to cry out. I wanted no more alcohol, no painkillers, nothing. Yet because of all the monitors, the staff could tell from my vital signs that I was in pain, and more contractions were triggered by that pain. I tried to deny it when confronted, but the nurse had a syringe full of morphine and insisted that without it I would not be able to keep from going into premature labor.

"All right, but the only way I'll take it is if you give me half what you have in that syringe right now."

She emptied half of it, and even with a half dose, I hallucinated for hours, seeing wheat growing and bugs crawling in the room. When I was finally out of danger and was wheeled back down the hall, my IV fluid bottle fell and smashed on the floor. Within seconds I was flooded with pain and felt a severe contraction. They rushed me the other way and set me up with a new IV that eventually took me out of danger. I absolutely refused any more morphine. It masks symptoms and fools the body, and I believe Clebe healed better and faster than most of his fellow patients because he also refused morphine; while many of the others were in dreamland and looking forward to their next shot, his body was working on healing itself.

The next day when I woke up, Betsy Richardson and Betty Fisher were at my bedside. "Everybody's been praying for you, Deanna—the whole crusade team and even the people who attended. Clebe was too shaken up to be able to speak, so they got a substitute, but he's okay now."

"Where *is* Clebe, Betsy?"

"Oh, he and Bobby are in a celebrity softball game today."

I couldn't believe Clebe would neglect me in my hour of need after all I had done for him. I knew he hated funerals and hospital scenes, especially when someone is at his lowest point. I knew it made his injuries burn more, depressed him, got to him, but you know what? I didn't care. I needed him when I was hurting, in pain, suffering. I *wanted* him to have the same concern for me as I had for him. I thought he would.

I had seen him at the precipice of death, and our bonding was incredible. I assumed he would respond the same way with me. But he didn't. And I didn't deal with it. When I saw him next, I questioned him and told him how hurt and disappointed I was, but we never resolved it. I eventually swept it under the rug.

Clebe's speaking engagement at the crusade was put off until that Sunday, when evangelist Leighton Ford (Billy Graham's brother-in-law) was to preach. When Reverend Ford heard Clebe, he encouraged Dr. Graham to invite Clebe to one of his crusades. Before we knew it, Clebe had been invited to Dr. Graham's October 1969 Anaheim Crusade. Clebe, of course, accepted immediately.

I was terrified. That was when our baby was due. Most any wife would be thrilled to think her husband could minister with Billy Graham, but I was just certain the baby would come while he was gone. I was starved for Clebe's concern. That made me a fearful weakling, not a giver. I wanted my way and my will, no matter how that fit in with God's will, but I wasn't selfish on purpose. My heart needed the nourishment of Clebe's loving attention.

Of course, it's natural to want your husband with you when you're delivering your child, but I should have had the peace that God would work it out. Our baby was two weeks late, Clebe was very effective on the program, and thousands came to Christ.

On October 22, 1969, Tara Deanna was born. And she was perfect. Healthy. Beautiful from the inside out. She still is. Doctors had warned me she might never be normal due to the accident, my trauma, and hers. They were right. She's not normal. She's extranormal!

With a baby in the house, Clebe and I got a taste of what our lives would be like from then on. Of course, we knew Tara would grow up and become independent, and we hoped to have at least one more child. But family life was something altogether different from just the two of us in an unusual marriage. There are many things I do to this day for Clebe. But suddenly I was being called upon to care for Clebe and someone else.

When he dresses up, Clebe often wears a dress shirt. If he is in uniform, as he frequently is while speaking, we're talking countless buttons. It's almost as hard to unbutton those as it is to button them, so whenever possible, I assist on both ends of that operation. Clebe has a little tool to assist with buttons when I can't be with him, but it's still a tiresome ordeal. He's persistent to the point of stubbornness, however, and he'll stick with buttoning till it's done, whether I'm with him or not.

Simple, ordinary, everyday things most of us take for granted are challenges to Clebe. Try to put on a sock with one hand, a hand with only two functioning fingers. Write a check. Tie a tie. Fasten a belt. Tie a shoe. Cut a piece of meat. Remove a napkin ring. Serve a tennis ball. Whenever I'm with Clebe, I'm honored to do as many such things for him as I can.

Once when I was fixing dinner, Clebe let me know that Tara smelled as if she needed a change.

"Be right there!"

But I wasn't right there. I got involved with a recipe, and Clebe began to sympathize with Tara. He checked, and sure enough, she needed changing. He called for me again and I put him off again, so he took matters into his own hand. He tried getting the disposable diaper off, but the tape tabs were stubborn, as they often are for those of us with two hands. With her dirty diaper half on and half off, poor Tara had to be miserable; Clebe decided he couldn't wait for me. He secured her on the bed, then ran and turned on the shower, returned to get her, and held her under the warm stream. That accomplished two tasks at once. The diaper slid off and fell to pieces in the shower, and Tara was squeaky clean. Clebe was proud of himself. I had quite a mess to clean up in the shower, though.

One thing Clebe did with both girls when they were little was to carry them around in a baby backpack. That was a big help to me, and I think it drew them closer to him, too.

Clebe and I were thrilled to have our first precious child, but little changed in our relationship. I still felt sorry for myself when I didn't get enough of his time. And that was often. I felt left out, excluded.

Clebe's work as a probation officer was frustrating, but most weekends he had the outlet of speaking here and there, sharing his testimony. I had been in a wheelchair after the baby arrived, and then graduated to crutches, but I still tried to go with him when I could. He was so well received that we couldn't understand why his parolees didn't appreciate him more. He finally realized that he could better serve those who came to him because they wanted to, not because they were required to meet with him.

After eighteen months on the job—and while I was pregnant with our second child—Clebe resigned and started a coffee house youth center in the basement of the old post office building in Georgetown. We got busy fixing that place up to try to reach troubled people of all ages in the Myrtle Beach, Grand Strand area.

Finally off crutches, I ignored the inconvenience of a new pregnancy and pitched in to help get the place in shape. Water had to be pumped out of the basement, the walls scraped and painted, and a whole lot of old-fashioned scrubbing done. We spent hours and hours, but I never complained. I learned to work from my daddy. Whatever his other faults were, and even though Mother might have tended to spoil me a little, Daddy taught me to work like a man. We kids had carried bricks, mowed, raked, shoveled, nailed, cleaned, painted, whatever needed to be done. We didn't have to like it. We just had to do it. It made us all better adults, I believe, and it made me intolerant of people who don't see a job that needs doing or who see it and don't just jump in and do it.

August 9, 1970, when I was about a month into my second pregnancy, Clebe and Tara and I were at a crusade in Manning, South Carolina. My little sister, Jennie, was along as a treat for her fourteenth birthday. The four of us were crammed into the front (and only) seat of Clebe's Ranchero (half car, half pickup). It was a rainy afternoon. We had just had Sunday dinner and were headed back to our hotel, less than a quarter of a mile away. Clebe was driving. Jennie was in the middle. I was on the passenger's side with Tara (nine months old) in my lap.

Two cars ahead of us slid and smashed into each other. Clebe slammed on the brakes, sending us into a slide right at them. It was as if those cars were careening back toward us! I screamed for him to stop, but there was nothing he could do.

In my mind I saw the police car from our first accident, then the Cadillac racing toward me. *Not twice! Not again!*

We plowed into those cars as I tried to cover Tara with my arms. On impact, Clebe's legs were thrust up under the steering wheel, Jennie was stunned when her forehead smashed the rearview mirror, and my head blasted into the windshield. Tara, unhurt but covered with bits of glass, screamed and screamed.

"Clebe! Are you all right?"

"My leg!"

"Jennie!"

She was dazed. The radiator spewed steam, and I feared the car was about to blow up. I jumped from the car with Tara in my arms, just as the passengers from the other cars and some passers-by approached. From the looks on their faces and their comments, I literally thought the top of my head had been ripped off.

"Oh, look at her!"

"Oh, no!"

"She's hurt bad!"

Someone yanked Tara out of my hands and insisted on getting me back into the car.

I called for my baby, but someone told me that she was in

good hands and I would see her at the hospital. I heard her screaming in the distance. Jennie was becoming more alert. Clebe was opening his door, eager to test his bruised leg. I pulled the rearview mirror toward me, and it fell to pieces in my hand. Holding a couple of the shards up to the light, I caught the reflection of myself, of the hideous monster that made strangers wince and pity me.

My forehead had swollen out several inches over my eyes, and I could see it by merely looking up. I can still hear the sound and feel the strange sensation when my head thudded against the windshield and that injury was inflicted. Whenever any of my family leave on a trip without me, I have a fear I have to surrender to God as those sensations come back to me. For years, our family traveled by bus, but I rarely slept well, listening for sounds of danger.

Two pregnancies, two accidents. No wonder I was apprehensive!

What sweet relief it was when I was reunited with Tara at the hospital. She was fine, just wailing for me. The doctor explained that because of protective fluids and nerve endings in the forehead, it's not uncommon to see the type of swelling I experienced with a solid knock to the head and a concussion. The swelling subsided in a few days, and I suffered no scars. Our injuries were minor, but I sure had been given a scare.

About twenty thousand people in the winter and two hundred thousand in the summer visited the Myrtle Beach Grand Strand. At the youth center we offered them an informal setting for Bible studies, just talking, Christian films, recreation, whatever. In a little over two years, we would meet more than six thousand people in that little place. The work was hard, and the results were slow, but it was rewarding.

Christa Annette came along April 5, 1971. Life with two little ones and a ministry was difficult for me. The biggest sacrifice I was called on to make was sometimes leaving my girls with their grandparents to travel and minister with Clebe. I cried and cried every time I had to leave them, visualizing home without me. When it was convenient, we took the girls, but frequently that was impossible. My heart longed to be with them, to hold them, to nurture them, and I could hardly wait to get home. As the girls began to walk and talk and become independent, I didn't discipline them properly. Whenever they needed correction, which was seldom, I barked commands. I felt as if I were in a pressure cooker. I was glad to have the girls for companionship, because I felt I hardly ever saw Clebe. In trying to keep up with his clothes, his schedule, his travel, dressing him, doing for him, I was frazzled.

Clebe had a lot to learn, of course, but so did I. The Lord had to work on me over the next several years, showing me, teaching me, working with me so I would learn. To have a caring, loving, understanding husband, I needed to be that kind of wife. Instead of demanding and insisting on compliance from my husband, I had to learn to be a giver, to be happy with my life. The rest would come, as it always does to those who are patient enough to leave the best choices to God.

I didn't know at that time that God was developing Clebe into an evangelist in his own right. He received so many invitations to speak that we realized more people could be reached through that kind of full-time ministry than we were able to affect in our little coffeehouse. We shut it down, and Clebe served part-time as an aide to Congressman Ed Young, counseling young people and speaking in high schools. Then Pastor Sam Anderson, the friend who had prayed with us when we received Christ on the infield of the stadium at McClenaghan High School in Florence, invited Clebe to speak at Teen Crusades all across America.

In September of 1973, we incorporated the Clebe McClary Evangelistic Association and began an exciting journey that continues to this day. You never know when you start something like that whether there will be enough invitations, enough ministry opportunities, to keep an association afloat. The fact is, it's been all we can do to keep up with the demand.

Clebe was speaking near Johnson City, Tennessee, and I had been asked to share my testimony and sing. Just before I was to share, a message was delivered. I ran to the phone to call home, then returned, trembling, to speak.

"I just returned from one of the most difficult phone calls I've ever had to make. Just a few minutes ago I was told there had been a call from the McLeod Infirmary in Florence. My grandfather, Arthur Fowler, has had a stroke."

The audience gasped.

"I just learned that Paw Paw is in intensive care and not expected to live through the night. I'm heartbroken. He has meant so much to me. He became a Christian before any of us, at the ripe age of seventy. Now, twelve years later, after praying Clebe and me into the kingdom, he lies at death's door.

"I know he would want us to continue to minister, so I want to tell you of Paw Paw Fowler and what a change occurred in his life when he gave his heart to Christ. He became a giver to the point that his own family thought he had become senile. At this very moment, he may be taking his last breath, but his future is secure. He's assured of a home in heaven. He's going to be with Jesus. Fortunately for him, he will not be one day too late. Will you?"

The audience was moved, still, quiet.

Choking back tears, I sang "One Day Too Late," then we drove all night to see Paw Paw. I'll always be grateful to God that He got us there in time. Paw Paw was still alive, but not for long. It gave me a chance to reminisce with him about the previous Christmas, one of the most precious times we had ever spent together.

CHAPTER 18

Hard Lessons

What a contrast between the dying Paw Paw and my memories of my grandfather—Arthur Bartley Fowler, Sr., the regal train engineer!

He lay there in the four-patient intensive care unit gasping for breath, his throat red. He stared at me, and no one could say whether he recognized me or would understand a word I said.

Later in my childhood, Paw Paw had become cross and cantankerous, especially with his grandchildren, but when he became a Christian, he was a new man, a generous giver. Now I stood before him, all grown up and married, a mother, a Christian. I took a swab from a nurse, volunteering to dab his throat the next time he needed it.

Because of the damage to Clebe's eardrums, I had grown accustomed to speaking loudly. And I knew Paw Paw was hard of hearing.

"Paw Paw," I said loudly, "I thank the Lord for your testimony and for what you've meant to us."

I broke down and couldn't go on. He half opened his mouth, so I swabbed his throat. He bit down on the stick and looked at me in a way that told me he not only knew who I was but also heard me and understood what I was saying. I was able to continue.

"Paw Paw, think of what they put in the Lord's mouth

when He was on the cross. You're realizing some of what Jesus went through. You're in His arms, and He loves you. Whatever happens, you'll be with Him. Paw Paw, you know what I have written here in my red Bible? It's my story of what happened last Christmas. Remember?"

I read him the story of how I hadn't known what to get him for Christmas. He had stored in his room every bottle of cologne or after shave, every necktie or pair of socks he had gotten over the years. The previous Christmas, we were at his home when I went to talk to him and found him kneeling in prayer by his bed.

I crept in and knelt next to him. He gave no indication he knew I was here, even when I prayed aloud and thanked God for him.

"Thank You, Lord, for Paw Paw, the kind of grandfather every girl needs. What a great example of prayer he's been to me."

When I slipped out, he stayed on his knees, having not spoken to me or acknowledged my presence.

The next morning when he came down for breakfast, he spoke to Goggie, "The greatest Christmas present I ever got I got last night from my granddaughter. Deanna knelt and prayed with me, and I don't think any other gift could ever top that."

I finished by praying for him and again thanking God for him. When I finished, he stared at me.

"Paw Paw, I know you can't speak. I just want you to know how much I love you."

A tear trickled out of his eye as the nurse came to usher me out. He died a couple of hours later, and I will always be convinced that he waited to die until he could see Clebe and me for the last time. He knew we would understand him and his relationship with the Lord. He was a special man.

Now, what was to happen to Goggie? Talk about a special person! For years she had cooked a huge Sunday dinner with three different kinds of meats and several vegetables, dozens of biscuits, cakes, pies, and anything else you could imagine—except cookies. Cookies were my specialty. She left those to me.

Anyone in the family (and several who weren't) was invited to Goggie's for those Sunday noon feasts. But now she was alone. She was heartbroken but always put up a stoic front. She rattled around in that big old empty house, and everyone assumed she would live with one of her sons or rotate between them. But she didn't. She loved our daughters and us so much that when we invited her to live with us, she didn't hesitate. For the next fifteen years until her death, Goggie lived in our home, helped raise our daughters, traveled with us, and was a central part of our family.

I know that such arrangements often don't work or they turn sour after awhile. For us, it was perfect. Goggie fit in from the beginning and was a tremendous help to me. None of us were perfect, and we didn't agree on everything, but we all feel that the fifteen years she was with us were the best of our lives. She was the first one up every morning, and when she rang a little hand bell in the kitchen, it was time for Tara and Christa to pad down and have their fresh, piping hot, homemade biscuits, made to order. To this day, the four of us mention Goggie frequently, and she's been dead for a few years already.

Goggie disagreed with me in the area of disciplining the girls, but she eventually saw that my way paid off. I shouldn't really say my way. The way I started out with the girls was a disaster. I felt like a verbal child abuser. And I've seen many other young mothers make the same mistake.

I was a Christian, and I wanted my children to be perfectly behaved. I told them what I wanted and what I didn't want, and when they acted contrary to that, I could hardly believe it. I knew they understood me. I knew they could remember. But sometimes they willfully disobeyed. I'm sure sometimes it was just childishness, but frequently, their actions required discipline. And so I scolded them. That grew into yelling. Threatening. Scowling. Making faces at them while yelling, which must have made me appear a monster to them.

I considered myself a failure as a mother, yet I was still enough of a perfectionist that I wanted to succeed. I continued to lay down the law, then scold and yell and sometimes, in public, I would quietly pinch their legs, while hissing out a threat.

"When we get out of here, you're really going to get it. I'm gonna spank you good."

Complicating my horrible technique was the fact that I never—fortunately—followed through on my threats. Of course, that would have been worse, but the girls eventually caught on to the fact that my threats were empty, so the threats became ineffective, too. I still feel guilty about those early failures, even though the problem has been rectified and the offenses forgiven. It always hurts when you've done your own children wrong.

One Sunday afternoon when the girls were three and four, I flipped on the television during their naps and watched D. James Kennedy preach from the Coral Ridge Presbyterian Church in Florida. He was speaking on proper biblical discipline and child rearing.

Wow, do I ever need that! Here I am, a Christian, and I don't know a thing about biblical discipline.

I had been trying to make my children look obedient in the eyes of the world. I knew nothing I was doing was right, and I began worrying about what I was doing to their inner beings. I wondered if they could ever grow up to be true Christians if I broke their spirit with all my yelling and threatening. I succeeded only in scaring them and convincing them I was unhappy with their behavior. But their natures and behavior patterns weren't changing. In fact, as they realized that the worst they were going to get was a raised voice, they saw misbehavior in a different, less serious light. They had to wonder, however, if their Mommy really loved them unconditionally.

A light went on in my head and heart that afternoon as I heard Dr. Kennedy talk about proper discipline. He advocated spanking for willful disobedience. He urged warning a child clearly so she knows precisely what is expected of her, then a careful, reasoned, nonviolent, calm judgment on the part of the parent when there is clear disobedience. He recommended using a paddle or some other simple instrument that would not injure the child, advising against using the same hand that loves the child to punish her.

I was so intrigued and encouraged, I sent for a copy of a brochure the TV ministry offered, "Children: Fun or Frenzy?" Frenzy was my middle name, so I read that booklet over so many times I nearly memorized it, and I've distributed hundreds since then. It changed the way I raised my girls, and it worked wonders.

Goggie didn't like it at first. We were ministering in Arizona when the girls acted up on our bus, and I made it clear they were not to do it again. When they misbehaved, I calmly planned to spank them in private, over the protests of their great-grandmother.

"Deanna, I can't stand children being spanked. If you spank them, I won't be riding back to South Carolina with you."

But I knew I was right. "Goggie, it's a long walk."

The girls begged me not to spank them. They made promises that would have convinced a hangin' judge. But that's the way we had lived for too long. I told them what they had done wrong, I told them how many swats they would get—where it would sting but not really hurt them—and I told them I loved them and wanted them to learn to obey.

After the girls finished crying and thinking about what they'd done, they sought me out to re-establish contact, to get back the old mother-daughter relationship. I hugged them and told them how much I loved them, then prayed with them. (And Goggie rode back home with us.) The girls were sweethearts for weeks, until the next incident. There were several more spankings over the years, but never in anger. No more yelling. No more threats. No more harried Mom, at least in the discipline department.

As the girls grew out of diapers and playpens, we began to take them on the road with us more and more frequently. We carried them onstage before they were each a year old, and when they could walk, we coaxed them out to say their name or a verse or even to sing with Mommy. Clebe doesn't sing, but he enjoyed introducing his "three girls" to sing for the people.

For many years we wondered what to do with Christa because she couldn't carry a tune. Yet she loved to sing in public. Eventually, we asked sound people to balance our mikes so she wouldn't really come through, but one night we got there too late to do any sophisticated mixing. We simply had the man turn off Christa's microphone, but then, because she couldn't hear herself, she sang even louder.

Finally I realized that I couldn't worry about her professionalism. After all, she was a little girl who loved Jesus and wanted to make a joyful noise, so we just let her sing. I was afraid she would grow up tone deaf, and I prayed that God would allow her to sing and enjoy it.

I'll never forget the night when she was about thirteen and she came to me with a song she wanted to sing as a solo— "Friends Are Friends Forever If the Lord's the Lord of Them." I was hesitant to encourage her, but I didn't want to deprive her of the joy. I nearly wept when she sang with power and beauty, every note right on pitch. Later, when she learned that I had been praying for years that God would allow her to sing, she was surprised.

"Mother, you never told me I *couldn't* sing!"

Now, because of all those years of her trying to be heard through a dead microphone, she has the most powerful voice in the family and doesn't even need a mike in most situations.

I try to keep from bragging about my daughters, but for the most part, I don't have to brag because others do it for me. From their friends, their teachers, their relatives, people at church, anyone who knows them, we hear accolades constantly. Most people tell us that Tara and Christa are the sweetest, most friendly, loving, polite, industrious teen-agers they have ever met.

When each girl reached thirteen, Clebe asked her out for a date. He was the first date for both of them, and we made a major production of it. I let the girls shave their legs for the first time, took them shopping for clothes, and did their hair and makeup just so. Clebe handled everything with formality, being polite, giving them flowers, opening doors for them, the works. They just glowed at the attention.

Clebe took pictures and bragged to waiters that his daughter had turned thirteen and that this was their first date. Then they would drive down to the ocean for father-daughter talk. He told them what to look for in a man and what men appreciate about women. He also asked them what they would change about him, if they could.

Of course, the point of the whole evening was that no boy should ever treat them with less respect and honor than he did. He still takes the girls out on dates on their birthdays every year.

People might assume that as soon as they're out of our sight, these two live it up and do everything we forbid at home. But we know otherwise. They were known at Georgetown High School for their faith, their standards, and their beautiful personalities.

Despite the fact that they don't go to offensive movies, use bad language, drink, or smoke, they were favorites among their friends and were voted Miss Georgetown High, Tara one year and Christa the next. In 1988 Tara was chosen South Carolina National Teenager from a field of seventy-two contestants, who also chose her Miss Congeniality. Tara now attends Furman, and Christa is at Clemson. We sent them off with confidence, but the girls also had the confidence that I would visit them often.

I know that getting my act together in disciplining the girls was good for them, but it was also good for me, which made it good for Clebe and our marriage. I became a much calmer mother and wife. Instead of always feeling under pressure, behind schedule, frustrated, and angry, I was finally disciplined myself. I still had a lot to learn about being a good wife, but that helped me get a head start in trying to be more understanding, patient, and tolerant.

Clebe began to use me more and more in the ministry, since he believes I complement him. When he runs into a situation he feels I can handle better, he turns it over to me. Probably the most well-known case was that of Harold Morris. Harold was the most outstanding athlete at Winyah High School, a three-sport standout and all-state basketball teammate of Clebe's graduating a year ahead of him in 1959. Harold fell in with the wrong crowd and wound up at the wrong place at the wrong time. He was convicted and sentenced to life in prison for armed robbery and murder (his story is told in the Focus on the Family book and film *Twice Pardoned*).

In February of 1974, Clebe visited Harold in the Georgia State Penitentiary near Reidsville. Clebe wept for Harold as he saw how lonely and scared and defeated he had become. Harold maintained his innocence, but there seemed little hope of release. Clebe talked with him about the Lord and left a Bible with him but felt he wasn't getting through to Harold. Clebe thought he needed a gentler approach: mine.

Clebe was wrong about the impact he had made on Harold. Harold tells the story of noticing that a Marine, a man who had suffered seven different wounds in war, had shed a tear for him. Still, Clebe wanted me to talk to Harold personally. I wasn't so sure about that.

"Clebe, I've never been in a prison. Is it safe? Harold doesn't even know me. What can I do or say?"

He assured me it was safe, but I wasn't prepared for the sights and sounds and smells at Reidsville. What a horrible, depressing place! I went in alone to a prison full of rough, catcalling men. I felt uncomfortable, knowing they were all staring at me. But I knew I was meant to be there. I also knew that though we might never see Harold again, we could have the Lord's Word to transform his life.

As soon as I saw Harold, I wrapped my arms around his neck and told him we loved him. He was stunned to silence. I assured him of our interest and wrote several references for him to look up later.

"Promise me you'll read these, Harold."

"I will."

"Promise me."

He smiled.

"I promise."

If we confess our sins, He is faithful and just to forgive us our sins and to cleanse us from all unrighteousness (1 John 1:9).

Who Himself bore our sins in His own body on the tree, that we, having died to sins, might live for righteousness—by whose stripes you were healed (1 Pet. 2:24).

For the wages of sin is death, but the gift of God is eternal life in Christ Jesus our Lord (Rom. 6:23).

Behold, I stand at the door and knock. If anyone hears My voice and opens the door, I will come in to him and dine with him, and he with Me (Rev. 3:20).

I asked Harold to read those verses. Then I encouraged him to keep reading them in the Bible Clebe had left with him. I also left him a tape of Clebe's testimony.

"Clebe and I love you, and we're going to pray for you. God will help you."

When I rejoined Clebe outside the prison in the parking lot, he felt led to kneel and pray for Harold before we drove away, unaware that Harold could see him.

Harold told cellmates that the only man who had ever cried over him had also knelt to pray for him. God had put several other key people in Harold's path before we helped harvest the seed they had planted, and that night Harold was miraculously and wonderfully saved, pardoned from his sin and, eventually, from prison. He is one of God's choice servants today, speaking all over the country to young people and pointing them toward Jesus.

Learning that the spotlight didn't satisfy but that being a giver, a true minister, was my only source of real fulfillment helped me come to terms with my role. The more I gave, the more I wanted to give, and the more I cooperated and encouraged Clebe, the happier and more satisfied I was. I quit fighting him and his schedule, and I became a partner in the ministry.

Late in 1974, Arthur Chastain, a young singer, joined our team and sang with me in meetings. He did most of the bus driving for us, which was a big break for Clebe, but more important, he had real musical talent. We recorded several albums together, and he was a joy to have with us for a few years until being away from his family so much got to be too much of a strain. He had logged a lot of miles with Clebe and the girls and Goggie and me.

Later I would become known more as a soloist in my own right. I recorded several albums and was even nominated for two Dove awards. That proved to be a very frustrating period for me, even though I rubbed shoulders with a lot of famous people and got all and more of the attention I had always thought I wanted. It was as if the Lord were saying, in essence, "Is this what you want, for people to see you for yourself and not as someone's wife?"

The fact is, when I was in the limelight, I hated it. Interested parties recommended that I go by just my first name on one of my albums, and that simple decision made me feel almost unfaithful to Clebe. I sang songs other people wrote for me or encouraged me to sing; I cut records they wanted cut; I sang where and when they wanted. Suddenly, I was Deanna, the gospel recording artist. That may, at one time, have been what I thought I wanted, but shortly I had had enough. I was Deanna McClary, emphasis on the *McClary.* I was Clebe McClary's wife, emphasis on the *wife.* I was born, raised, chosen, called, and ordained to be Mrs. Clebe McClary, not Deanna.

I still sing, I still record, but no one calls me simply Deanna. I have a personal ministry of counseling and speaking and singing, but first and foremost Deanna's story is Clebe's story. My ministry is his ministry. I support him, aid him, try to make his life easier. It's where I feel most comfortable, most secure, most productive. It fits me. It feels proper. It feels great!

When I voluntarily took a back seat and quit trying to project myself into the spotlight, God began to use my humble offerings. He blessed my singing and my counseling, but the real surprise was His using me as a speaker, in my area of greatest weakness, which is just like Him.

CHAPTER *19*

Terror

*T*he persistence and boldness that allowed God to use me as a witness and a counselor for Him also contributed to my being a complainer who almost drove my husband into retreat. The day would come when I would realize that complaining was a dead-end street. Complaining didn't work. Clebe never gave in to me; he tuned me out and did what he had to do, which eventually showed me that I needed a new tack. In witnessing, however, persistence and boldness paid off.

In the late 1970s, Clebe and I were flying back from meetings out West when he told me he wanted to get some rest and wanted me to do the same.

"I want to sack out, so don't be runnin' your mouth."

That statement wasn't as cold as it sounds. He smiled when he said it. That's one loving way he communicates with me. We both know I have a tendency to run my mouth. I agreed with him. I was tired anyway. But when our meals came, I noticed a gaunt soldier across the aisle, in uniform, not eating, pushing his food around the plate. I studied his eyes. I saw emptiness, frustration. I couldn't hold back.

I tried to strike up a conversation with him, but I couldn't get him to even introduce himself. So, I leaned across the aisle and talked for two solid hours, telling him all about myself, my life, Clebe, our faith, our struggles, our victories. I told him that no matter who he was, what he had done or not done, what his successes and failures were, God loved him.

He wouldn't respond. I told him he reminded me of myself several years earlier.

"You're all torn up inside, aren't you?"

I was oblivious to how loud I had been. I glanced behind me to find people leaning out into the aisle, listening. Strangers had heard everything and knew as much about my life as I did. I was stunned when the plane began to descend, the time had sped so quickly. I felt like a babbling idiot, because for the entire two hours, my intended audience (the undernourished soldier) had refused to look at me or to respond. He had a this-lady's-a-loony look on his face. I handed him a Bible.

"It has our name and address in it. We care about you. We love you, and if you ever feel like talking, get in touch with us. Most important, remember the Lord Jesus loves you."

We were running late, so we hurried off the plane, and I jogged to catch up with Clebe. As we emerged from the jetway into the bright lights of the terminal, I heard a voice behind me.

"Ma'am! Ma'am! Just a minute! Please! I have to talk with you."

It was the young soldier. He was tall and so thin his uniform hung on him. I saw tears. Clebe stood off to the side, my clue that he was willing to wait while I finished my conversation with the young man.

"I'm sorry, ma'am, but I have to talk to you now. You seemed to know all about me, yet I know I don't know you and you don't know me. I know I didn't seem interested in a thing you were saying, but I heard every word you said. You're right. I'm torn up inside. My mom and dad have kicked me out of the house because I'm hooked on drugs. I'm on drugs because I saw my buddies all blown apart in Vietnam. Me and a couple of other guys survived the attack, but I can't get the horror of the memory out of my mind. It's all I see when I'm not high. It's all I dream about at night. The reason I couldn't eat tonight is the same as the reason I haven't had a full meal for months. I don't have any desire for food.

"But today I had come to a decision. I didn't want to go

on anymore. When I got back to the barracks, I was going to blow my brains out. But when you told me God loved me, it reminded me of when I was a little boy and I went to Sunday school every week. I heard then that Jesus loved me, and it seemed real. Lately it's seemed like a fairy tale. I can tell He's real to you, because you cared enough to tell me all about Him, even when I was being rude. Would you pray with me? I want to do what you said and receive Jesus into my life."

I had been unaware of all the people passing as we spoke, but his request that I pray with him brought me back to reality. I suddenly thought how bright the terminal was and how many people would notice us praying in public.

What will people think? This is foolish. But as quickly as that thought came, I was reminded of those same thoughts the night I tried to talk myself out of going forward to receive Christ.

"I want to go somewhere with you to pray, but I don't guess we have a place or the time. Let's look at this spot right here as God's delivery room. I'm just here to assist Him in your birth into His kingdom. I'm the midwife. I'm going to pray, and I want you to repeat after me. And I want you to believe in your heart that the Lord Jesus took your sin and guilt and that they were nailed to the cross with Him, where He died for you, that He was buried, and that He rose again. It's not me, but Christ in me who wants you to come into His eternal kingdom, to forgive you of your sin, to give you abundant life that never ends."

Clebe came over and put his arm around me as the young man responded.

"Yes, ma'am. I'm ready."

I prayed, and he repeated the sinner's prayer. When he finished, he hugged us, sobbing. We never heard from him again. My prayer is that many other veterans will finally release their guilt and surrender to a new life in Christ.

In the late 1970s, during a brief period when Clebe and I made an ill-fated attempt at opening and running a restaurant on

Hilton Head Island, Clebe began to hear roaring sounds in his head. We were both working hard. I figured he was just exhausted. Occasionally he would ask if I heard a train. There are no trains on Hilton Head.

"I've got a bad headache," he said.

I believed him, but there was little I could do for him. Clebe never wanted to go to the doctor for fear of hospitalization. The best I could do was to encourage him to take something for it. He would not slow down, would not quit working, would not take a break, Finally, however, I could tell by looking into his eyes that this was something serious.

"Clebe, there is something wrong with you."

"Now, don't be tellin' me that."

"I'm not trying to worry you, darling, but you need to see a doctor. I want to scare you into going, if that's what it takes. You don't look good."

He wouldn't go. "I'll be okay."

But then I noticed him pulling away. He found reasons to withdraw from people. Rather than mingling and working inside, he'd be out mowing the lawn while I ran things inside. That wasn't like him. He had been a people person all his life. We had built this restaurant, and now both of us hated it. It wasn't for us. We would last just fifty-two days, but Clebe never would have given up that soon if it hadn't been for our physical ailments. Stress caused me to develop gastritis. Something else caused problems for Clebe. He was about to leave for a weekend to speak in Oklahoma City, but when he got up, he suffered from vertigo.

"I can't even put a foot on the floor, Dea!"

"Then get back in that bed."

"I'll be all right. Just let me sit here a minute. Gotta keep goin'."

Providentially, Dr. Jack Hough, an ear specialist, practiced in Oklahoma City and was involved with the group to which Clebe was speaking. Clebe let Dr. Hough check his ears.

"Clebe, you've got a hole in your ear, a perforated eardrum."

"I've had that for a long time, Doc."

"Let me fix it. I think I can do a better job on it."

Clebe told him that he was going from Oklahoma to Spokane as planned, but he promised he'd let Dr. Hough operate on him when he got back. It was to be a routine cleansing of the area and repairing of the perforation. It would be the first stateside operation on Clebe that I would not attend, but it was simple enough, and had I been informed about it, I would have encouraged it.

Of course, Dr. Hough didn't know that Clebe's speaking tours sometimes take in a dozen or so schools a day, plus churches and whatever else he can work in. By the time Clebe returned to Oklahoma City, he was exhausted, yet he fulfilled several engagements there before Dr. Hough admitted him for surgery.

Clebe called me when it was over to tell me about it, and my first thought was that I had missed my special place at his side. I was relieved, though, because everything was fine, and I knew he had needed something to be done. I heard later from the doctor, however, and he told me the whole story.

"I thought the hammer, anvil, and stirrup had been replaced before, but I found bits and pieces of them. As I cleaned out the area and planned to replace the bone where necessary, we found a tumor at the base of the brain in the mastoid. That's the worst place, and it had not shown up on the x-ray. Had we not discovered it and removed it, it would have killed him within a year."

I wept. How much is a person supposed to endure? Clebe's recuperation and recovery took longer than usual. We got out of the restaurant business pronto, and we have been full-time in the Lord's work ever since.

I have always tried to help Clebe and not act like a weakling. I'm not too proud to do men's work when necessary, and when I want to move furniture around, I don't wait until Clebe is home. Sometimes I get in the mood to rearrange a room when he's away. When he gets home, he doesn't have to ask anymore who moved the couch and chairs and tables.

Clebe once had more than sixty long pier poles shipped to us—the gigantic wood posts used to support landing docks. His plan was to dig holes for them about five feet deep in the back yard, and then tip those several-hundred-pound poles up on end and into the ground. It's grueling work for several men, let alone for one man with one arm and a heavy, complicated, prosthesis. Not only that, this man had too much pride to let his wife help. I wanted to take some of the strain and agony off him. I watched as he struggled bare chested in the sun, maneuvering that bulky artificial arm with its figure-eight wires across his back.

Sweat cascaded down his scarred spine—which to me serves as a map of the route he took from the pungi pit to the ground under the force of those Viet Cong satchel charges. Whenever I see those deep scars along his riddled spine, I picture him flying through the air like a limp doll, head flung one way, legs another.

Working with a post hole digger is tough for anyone, driving the parallel shovel blades as deep as you can, then yanking the handles apart to scoop the dirt. That's the easy part. Then you have to lift, with the handles still apart, turn and pile the dirt out of the way. All those actions and reverse actions take concentration and work when you're working your fake arm by twisting your shoulders.

I saw the pain and strain in his face, but all I could do was watch. In half a day he got three holes dug—imagine him leaning over narrow, five-foot deep holes, pulling the last scoops out and away. How he got those poles in the right position and tipped them up and in, I'll never know. I could see how good this landscaping project was going to look, but I wondered how long it would take.

The next day he left for a three-day speaking trip. I knew it was foolhardy, but I headed straight for the back yard and the post hole digger. Drive down, push, pull, lift, push back together, hour after hour in the blazing sun. I sweated, I ached, I groaned, but there was nothing in the world I'd rather have been doing because this was a gift to my husband who deserved everything I had to offer.

At the end of two days I had dug all the holes and wrestled in the sixty-plus poles. I could hardly believe it myself. I still have the hernia I caused that second day, but it was worth it for the look of wonder and admiration on Clebe's face when he got home. He simply couldn't believe it. He made a great effort to act angry with me for overexerting and doing strenuous work, and I took some criticism from my mother who said I risked leaving Clebe with no one to look after him.

But I'd do it again in a minute. I owe it to my father that I don't shrink from hard work, and there's not a better gift you can give a loved one than to do a difficult task for him.

One night about midnight the next year, Goggie and Clebe and the girls and I were on Pawley's Island after having taken one of our girls' friends home. I was driving. We had seen no other cars on the road when I saw a vehicle with flashing headlights race up behind us.

He must be in an awful hurry.

I wondered why he didn't just pass me. I was in the right lane. Instead he pulled behind me and tapped my bumper. Now I was sure it was an emergency. I pulled off the road to let him get by, but he pulled in behind me and bumped me again!

"Clebe! He's after us!"

Clebe wrenched around in the seat, scowling and trying to get a look at our pursuer. From the height of the headlights and the sound of the vehicle, we could tell it was a four-wheel-drive truck, jacked up all the way around.

"Step on it, Dea. Let's get outta here!"

I pressed the accelerator and threw gravel behind us as I fishtailed onto the highway again. Goggie kept the girls quiet as I studied the road and the rearview mirror, and Clebe kept an eye on the chasing car. I feared for the lives of my family, and when I saw the little Pawley's Island Apothecary, I swerved into the parking lot. The truck nearly overran us again, but I prayed he would leave us alone when we got off the highway and out of the way.

As soon as I got into the parking lot, the truck—which we could now see was red—whipped around in front of us and stopped. The apothecary was dark, and still there was not another car on the road. I felt helpless, but I was mad. And I was a mother hen. I was not going to just sit there and let some maniac terrorize my family. My husband, wounded for his country, sat beside me. My two little daughters were in the back seat with my precious grandmother. I felt I had to show strength.

I threw the car into reverse, backed up several feet, and flew out onto the highway again, getting a several-hundred-yard lead on the truck. But he hadn't given up. With its powerful engine, that red vehicle soon caught us and came alongside on the right. The driver swerved toward my door as if to push me off the road.

"Clebe! What am I going to do?"

I was going too fast and had too much on my mind to be able to look at Clebe, but I heard him loud and clear. He rarely raises his voice or speaks in anger, so when he does, I listen.

"Stop the car, right now!"

At that instant, I was overwhelmed with gratitude that I was married to a tough and brave and take-charge man. I began to pull off the road.

"Don't pull off! Just stop right here."

"Right here on the highway?"

"Yeah."

When I slammed on the brakes, the truck slid sideways and almost hit us. Then it pulled in front of us again, and the driver got out. Clebe jumped out, and we finally got a look at the driver of that red terror machine. He was huge with a full beard and hair tumbling out from under his cap. I rolled down my window. Clebe confronted the man.

"What are you tryin' to do? Can't you see I've got my wife and family and a grandmother in that car? You tryin' to kill us or somethin'? Are you crazy, man?"

When the big man heard *crazy*, he strode back to his truck. If he'd made a move toward Clebe, I'd have run over him. Clebe thought he had scared him off and turned back to the car. But from where I sat—and Goggie had a good view, too—I could see the man was not climbing back into his truck but was reaching under his seat. I envisioned him firing a gun into our car to get back at the man who had hassled him.

I screamed, "Clebe! Get in quick! He could have a gun! I'm leaving!"

Clebe skipped into the car and I tore out of there as he was shutting the door. I didn't hesitate or strategize. I put the accelerator down until the needle flirted with a hundred miles an hour. Within a minute, the truck was next to me again, but this time we were both going a lot faster than before. There was no margin for error. Clebe turned to me.

"Honey, if he hits us, we're gone."

Worse, I imagined he was aiming a pistol at us as we rocketed down the highway. Any second I expected to hear a shot or feel a bullet or see glass shattering near my loved ones. I edged forward and pointed my toe so the accelerator was ironed against the floorboard.

I knew where I was headed. The fire station wasn't far away. I just had to decelerate precisely so I could get into the entrance and be able to run my family inside. But I needed more distance between him and me. I left that pedal down until the engine was roaring in protest.

Suddenly, as we neared the fire station, the truck wheeled around in the middle of the road. I turned into the drive and we ran into the station. Clebe and I reported what had happened, and a fireman said he would inform the police.

We drove home shaken, but grateful the Lord had protected us. The girls were petrified, but as we got into the house, Goggie and I tried to explain that we had simply been dealing with a wild man who wouldn't be able to scare us any more. I wasn't as confident as I sounded, but I wanted to reassure them so they wouldn't have nightmares.

Clebe looked whipped. It hadn't been that long since his brain tumor operation, and this had been as much strenuous activity as he had had in a long time.

"I gotta get to bed."

He trudged up the stairs, and I knew that as soon as his

head hit the pillow he would be out and unable to hear another sound. His hearing was bad enough, besides the fact that he slept so soundly.

As Goggie and the girls and I stood in Goggie's apartment (attached to the house by a glassed-in breezeway) and tried to calm one another, I heard an engine, and bright lights flooded the room. I turned in horror as I recognized the red truck, pulling onto our property. I wrenched the drapes across the breezeway and told the girls to hit the floor and crawl to the closet. As soon as the drapes were shut, the man banged on the glass door. I didn't dare try to get past the door to wake up Clebe. I was convinced the man had a gun.

I crawled to the phone and prayed that God would help me remember a little dialing technique that allowed phone users to make their own phones ring (unfortunately, that ability no longer exists). While I was frantically praying and thinking about it, I did it instinctively. It took the phone awhile to penetrate Clebe's unconsciousness, and I'm sure he wondered where his wife was and why she didn't answer the phone. Finally, he picked up the receiver.

"Clebe, get down here fast. . . . that guy's here and he's about to break down our door."

"I'll bring the gun."

I heard Clebe rustling around upstairs as I called both the sheriff and the highway patrol.

"There's a madman at our house. He tried to run us off the road earlier tonight, and now I think he has a gun and is trying to break into our house."

I pleaded with Clebe to wait for the law officers, but he was mad. He took his pistol and went straight for the glass door. I prayed like never before that Clebe wouldn't get himself shot and leave us helpless. He was taking charge.

"What's your problem, man? Get away from my house and off my property!"

The man was enraged, his eyes wild and blazing. "You reported me tonight, man! Why'd you do that?"

"What're you talkin' about, son? You could have killed us

all on the highway, driving like that. What'sa matter with you anyway? You crazy?"

"You lied! I haven't done anything to you! I'll get you for this!"

"You won't touch a member of my family or you'll regret it."

It seemed like hours before the officers arrived, but it was only minutes. The man admitted that he had been drinking and doing drugs because his girl had dumped him. He was mad and was going to take it out on whoever was available. We had simply been in the wrong place at the wrong time.

It took a long while for our family to feel comfortable in our own home again. That's the tragedy of such incidents. I hated what that man had done to us and to our little girls' sense of security. But Clebe and I drew closer because of it. A certain bonding takes place when a husband and wife go through a crisis together, especially one that involves the defending of a home and family.

Our children are the only blood relatives the two of us share, of course, and we feel a heavy responsibility for them. I was slowly learning, too, that the more I did *with* Clebe, not just *for* him, the stronger our marriage became. And the more I encouraged, backed, and supported him, the better a husband he became.

CHAPTER 20

Growing Character

My pursuit of true knowledge about my husband has made me a better wife and has given us a marriage solid and indivisible. My motives have changed. My methods have dramatically changed. I used to complain and badger, always interested in changing him, but I have come to see that if I support him, I am fulfilled.

I'm not saying he was always in the right and I was always in the wrong. What I am saying is that he usually had pure motives, even when he was wrong. If he was insensitive, he didn't mean to be. If he was stubborn or cold, he was never cruel, never mean. I sometimes misinterpreted his actions, but I soon learned I was wrong.

When I began affirming him, backing him, supporting him, truly helping him, I understood him better than ever. I learned some of that from Goggie. We were blessed in many ways to have her in our home, but had the only benefit been what I learned about my husband, it would have been worth it.

I used to call him at his office, just a short drive from our home, and tell him to pick up a few things at the store on his way home. It irritated me that he didn't cheerfully agree. He either begrudgingly said okay or asked me why I couldn't do it myself. I considered such errands part of his marital duty. When he forgot or made a mistake in my order, I took it personally. I knew he didn't really want to do it, so I accused him of having forgotten or fouled up on purpose.

Goggie knew better, but it took me years of observing to learn the lesson. So, how did Goggie get through to Clebe? Here's an example:

"Clebe, honey, I'm gonna be makin' a fresh salad for dinner tonight, but all I have is lettuce. I don't know anybody who loves a fresh garden salad the way you do, so will you bring me a few vegetables on your way home this evening?"

"Sure, Goggie! Whatcha want?"

"Oh, anything you pick will be perfect."

"Sprouts, carrots, that kinda thing?"

"Sounds wonderful, Clebe. I know you'll bring the best."

At first that about made me sick. I was jealous that Clebe seemed much more eager to do that for her than he ever had for me, but just passed that off on the fact that we're usually more polite to people outside the immediate family. Then I tried to justify it by the fact that Goggie had always sided with Clebe and thought he could do no wrong. She loved him like a son. She was layin' it on thick, and I thought he should have seen through it.

That evening, Clebe came home with a huge bag of groceries. Carrots, onions, celery, radishes, tomatoes, you name it, it went into that salad. He also bought some fresh bread and a few other goodies. Not only had he not forgotten, but he also brought home all she asked and more. I was amazed, but I kept telling myself she had done a number on him.

The more I talked to her, however, the more I realized that she had not been idly flattering him. She truly believed that Clebe appreciated good food, and she knew he would select just the right ingredients. By praising him with honest compliments, she made him feel good about helping. I know I always want to help someone when he tosses in a little sugar with the request. Instead of my *telling* Clebe that I needed him to do something the next time, I found something encouraging to say about him or to him, then I asked him nicely. He responded just as he had for Goggie, and the nicer I was to him, the nicer he was to me.

Rather than complaining and badgering about his hours or his schedule, I quit accusing him of neglecting us and started helping him stay organized. I told him how proud I was of his hard work and dedication and how pleased I was that he obeyed the Lord by speaking for Him where he was led. Without any great to-do, Clebe became more selective in his scheduling. He eventually set policies for how many days he would be away from the family, how many weekends a month he'd be away from our church, and when he would take one or more of us with him. I had been harping about those things for years. When I changed my attitude and methods, he came around. Once he turned down a particularly juicy pro football chapel assignment because he had set aside that week-end for the family, but within a week the Lord provided two even better ones that fit his new schedule.

The difference was dramatic. Clebe was the thoughtful, considerate, soft, kind man I married. That mellowed me im-mediately, and we were both rewarded for the way we treated and talked to each other. I know it's as simple as the golden rule and the soft answer that turns away wrath, so maybe it was our years of Bible study that helped us "stumble" onto these truths.

Meanwhile, I had grown confident, independent in the best sense, the best reflection of Clebe had encouraged me to be, even when he wasn't around. For years he had been trying to build me up, to tell me I had worth, to encourage me to be outgoing, to have my own interests.

Clebe has always been good with verbal affirmation. He seemed to appreciate everything I did. He told me I was the one who had given him the desire to live. Wow! What more could I do for him than that? You can imagine how that made me feel. That was a lot different from his telling me I looked beautiful. When he spoke of my beauty, he tore me apart with-out intending to.

I had been so concerned about beauty that his ravaging wounds taught me a lesson I could never forget; in fact, I could seldom turn away from the daily visual lesson I got. In spite of all his injuries, he was more beautiful than ever to me. He possessed that generosity, that giving nature, that acceptance.

I had to wonder if I could be that way if I had been disfigured. I had always been worried about what I looked like, certain that I could never look good enough. Now I loved a man for all that he was, minus physical perfection. Of course, as he healed, he was not repulsive to look at or to hold and kiss and love. People who see his shining good eye and his bright smile sense a picture of his youthful handsomeness. And I still think he is the most handsome of all.

But in the eyes of the world a man minus an eye and an arm is less than perfect, less than whole, less than beautiful. Yet I loved him so deeply that I knew it wasn't for his looks. Beauty had been my god. It had controlled every area of my life, my thoughts, my reactions, my emotions. Everything was controlled and dominated by whether I was accepted or rejected for my beauty or lack of it.

Clebe made me feel so urgently necessary and special that I began to grow out of that immature obsession with beauty. He was the perfect example of one who had been physically devastated, yet who remained beautiful from the inside out. That's what I wanted. I realized that whatever physical beauty I possessed could be taken away in an instant, but not the kind of inner beauty I saw in Clebe. I'm stuck in this aging, decaying body, and if all I have to offer Clebe is physical beauty, eventually he will lose interest. I want him to be able to look inside and find the part of me that can grow and develop and become better with the years, not the part that breaks down.

I looked for things I could do to develop the inner life. I become more willing to give, to share, to counsel, to love, to be hospitable, to become more spiritually mature. If Clebe notices and comments on those qualities, I am all the more fulfilled. The other kind of beauty is temporal, worldly, and destined to wane.

Many wives tell me that they could never have done for their husbands what I have done for mine. I find that shocking. People are always looking out for their own interests; that's why marriages break up. Spouses don't consider each other. They simply look at what they have to do that inconveniences them. I could wallow in self-pity. I could say that if I was married to someone else, he might be waiting on me and catering to me. I'd rather praise the Lord for the fact that I can do things for Clebe. That doesn't make me good. My life is full of joy and thanksgiving because of the opportunities God has given me to touch others as well as Clebe.

Clebe does all he can for me, from little things like filling my car with gas to big things like clearing his schedule for more family time. Whatever I can do for him just balances the picture and makes our love and marriage that much deeper.

As our daughters grew up and I interacted with Goggie every day, I found myself slowly becoming a different person. I lost my obsession with beauty, with my inferiority. God tuned my radar to people in need. I felt called to encourage, to bring out the best in people. Nothing pleases me more than to help a woman who has no idea of her beauty to look and feel better by helping her with her hair or makeup, while pointing her to her inner worth as a person.

I had also—again without knowing it—become a mother hen, defensive of my family, our safety, and my own safety. This instinct began to develop during my childhood years, protecting my brothers and sister and observing Mom's protective nature of us. I'm also confident the tendency was enhanced by my husband, though we never talked about it much. Akin to the feeling I had the night the drunk man tried to run us off the road, I guess I subconsciously thought I should always react the way Clebe would react, though I'm smaller and weaker.

One spring morning I decided I wanted a workout. One of my favorites is to walk in water up to mid-thigh, pushing against the force of the sea, which is as effective as working out with weights. I put on my blue one-piece suit of stretchy material that ties behind the neck. For some reason, instead of tying it in a bow as I had done countless times, I double-knotted it that morning. I threw on an old polyester shift for a beach covering and set out.

When I got to the water, I saw a few people near a hotel, but no one else on the beach. Just the way I like it. I took off my coverup and rolled it up, carrying it in one hand and my car keys in the other. I walked a couple of miles down the beach, then moved into the shallow water and headed back up the beach as briskly as possible. Holding my coverup and keys above the water line was good exercise, as was the walking itself.

I pushed slowly against the water, feeling it pull against my leg muscles. About a hundred yards up the beach I saw a man walking toward me. He was huge, shirtless, and tanned. He had long pants rolled up to mid-calf. Usually I look forward to happening onto strangers and greeting them, but something about this man made me feel uneasy. As he grew nearer I could see that his black hair was cut in a blunt, bowl-cut style. He was walking on the sand heading one way; I was in the water heading the other. As we passed I pretended to be studying the horizon and whistling lowly to cover the fact that I had not said anything.

Run! Get out of the water and run! Run!

I ignored that impulse. I felt it deeply, but I didn't want him to think I was scared. I didn't want to offend him. Why would I be running away from him all of a sudden?

I'm just being paranoid. This is insane.

I decided to just keep moving but to casually look back and see if he was still heading down the beach. He wasn't. He was in the water behind me. When he noticed me looking, he sat down, almost like a child playing in the water.

This is strange, Deanna. This is weird. Take off running! Now!

But I didn't. How could he have gotten from the beach to the water without my seeing or hearing him? I stepped up my pace and whistled more to appear unafraid. Just as I was about to sneak a peek to see if I had distanced myself from the sitting giant, he lunged for me and grabbed my thighs from behind, leaving ten black-and-blue marks where his fingers dug in. Once he had stopped me and I froze, he reached up with one hand, grabbed the back of my suit, and pulled it to my ankles.

Had he intended to rape me, he could have just tackled me and pushed me under the water. Yanking my suit down like that, exposing by backside, was the worst mistake he could have made. The material in my suit stretched almost to the breaking point and strained at my neck. Without losing my rolled-up shift or my keys, I held on at my neck so the suit would not give way. I reached back and pulled the suit back up, not screaming, not panicking. I spoke to him in a deliberate, firm, yet controlled, voice.

"Leave me alone! Do you understand? You leave me alone!"

He tried to pull the suit down again, but I had a vise grip on the material and wouldn't let him. He splashed around to the front and grabbed my suit, pulling as hard as he could. The doubled knot wouldn't budge, but it hurt against my neck.

All he wants to do is strip me. He's going to get a big charge out of embarrassing me in front of God and no one else. How insane of him to do this!

"Get away from me right now! Leave me alone! Get away from me now!"

I stared defiantly at him and held tightly to my suit. He gave up, finding me uniquely stubborn, and probably unsure what I might do next. He charged out of the water and up onto the sand and ran up the beach.

What was it that didn't allow me to simply thank God for protecting me? What was it that, yes, made me chase him? You read it correctly. I chased that man up the beach like a mad dog, screaming at him.

"I'm going to get you for this! You're going to be sorry!"

He was big and slow, lumbering up the beach, and I had the advantage of anger and adrenalin. I gained on him as he zigged and zagged and kept staring back at me in wide-eyed amazement.

"I'll get you!"

And then it hit me. *I'm going to catch this monster. Then what am I going to do?*

I should have slowed to a stop, yelled for help, but no one was near. I let him get away. I kept running. I knew he wasn't after me as long as I was after him. I needed to keep him scared of me. I was in control until we got to the sand dunes and he was suddenly on higher ground. That didn't deter me, though. I screamed at him.

"You are a very sick person! Do you know that? You're sick! In God's eyes, you need help! Now you get down here this minute! You owe me an apology! I mean it. Get down here right now! You owe me an apology for what you tried to do to me!"

Praise God, he didn't come down. He probably would have killed me. He stood above me, rocking back and forth and holding his head, as if in agony. I had no idea what was going on. At first I thought he was covering his face and pretending to be afraid, mocking me.

"There's no sense covering your face! I saw you, and I'm reporting you! You're never going to do this to another person!"

He waved disgustedly at me, turned and ran up into the trees out of sight into the new housing development. I quickly put on my coverup and ran down the beach to the hotel, screaming for help.

I ran to the hotel and pleaded with people there to call the police. When I told my story, the police officer announced that anyone with knowledge of the incident or the attacker should meet him downstairs. Ten of us showed up, all victims or friends of victims of the same man. I couldn't believe it.

"You were all attacked?"

Several nodded.

"Why didn't you report it?"

"We didn't want our names in the paper."

I couldn't believe that people could be so foolish. "Oh, so you just let him run free and attack unsuspecting people like me! How was I supposed to know there was a nut like that running around?"

Of course, like them, I was scared to death the man would retaliate. But this was my home! I wasn't about to let someone intimidate me and scare me out of my own town. I went all over that place, warning people, describing the man, seeking help in finding him and bringing him to justice. Amazingly, a woman and her young daughter saw the man coming after them over the dunes a few days later, and based on my description of him, they ran for help. Still he escaped.

Clebe had the best idea. After staking out the beach for a few days and nights, he decided that the man wasn't a resident. He was more likely a worker in the new housing development who stalked the beaches during his break. The roofers broke from 11:00 A.M. to 3:00 P.M. every day due to the heat.

The police investigated and interviewed a bunch of the workers and discovered one who fit my description. I had sketched the face as best I could remember it, but I dreaded identifying the wrong man. The police weren't sure they had the right one.

"He's a dead ringer for the description you provided, but he denies everything. He's threatening to sue us for false arrest. Would you take a look at him and identify him for us?"

I said I would try. To make sure he didn't take revenge on me, I took five women friends. As soon as I saw the suspect, I knew. It was him. As soon as he saw me, he confessed. He had been denying everything all along, but when our eyes met, he broke down.

Later, when he was being booked, I was asked to go to the station and sign the complaint against him. I was glad to do it, eager to protect the community from him. But when Clebe and I arrived in the parking lot of the police department, I had a bad feeling.

"What if he's sitting right out there in the open?"

"He's not. They wouldn't allow that."

"Check for me first, Clebe. Please."

"C'mon, Dea! You've got to sign the complaint."

"I'm not going in there. I don't want to be face to face with him again."

"Honey, he's in jail. He is *in* jail."

I made Clebe check, and sure enough, the suspect was

sitting right inside the door. Clebe couldn't believe it. He asked an officer to bring the papers out to the car. The sheriff walked out instead and told me he had some things to ask me. "He told me something I find very hard to believe, Mrs. Mc-Clary," the sheriff explained.

"What?"

"That you told him to apologize for what he tried to do to you. Did you say that?"

"Yes, sir. I'm not sure why, but I did."

The sheriff shook his head. "He says when you called him down, two voices spoke to him in his head. One told him to be very afraid of you and run, and the other told him that he *should* apologize. He's been in this kind of trouble since he was ten years old. He was really wrestling with himself."

(That was the reason he had rocked back and forth with his head in his hands on the sand dune.)

"I'm glad he listened to the first voice and didn't come down to apologize, because I would have died in my tracks."

I have never satisfied myself with an answer as to why I was so bold that day. I know I wouldn't have wanted to go down without a fight. Clebe had invested too much in me. I had learned so much from him, felt so sure and confident of his love. Maybe subconsciously I wanted to be just like him, a Marine who was afraid of nothing, who did what had to be done, who pushed himself to the limit every chance he got.

Never was that tenacity more developed and evident than when we found ourselves, just the two of us, battling nature in the mountains. It would be a holiday I would never forget.

CHAPTER 21

Mountaintop Experiences

*A*bout five years ago, Clebe and I visited dear friends in Colorado Springs: former Air Force Academy head football coach Ken Hatfield, who now coaches at Arkansas, and his wife, Sandy. We did a little hiking and picnicking in the mountains, but I had no idea Clebe was just warming me up to the climb he really wanted us to make. I loved being part of his world, and I would normally agree to just about anything to be with him, to stay by his side. He was independent and a doer, and although it would have been easier most of the time to let him do his own things, I knew he wanted me with him. That was all I needed to know. I wanted to be with him, too, no matter what the cost. Well, usually.

On the Fourth of July he awoke early, and he had that look in his eye. "Dea, honey, let's hike Pike's Peak today."

I didn't know Clebe had already confided in Ken Hatfield about his plans for the two of us that day. I was just proud of Clebe that he had that much energy and drive when he had lost so much in Vietnam. We both knew men who had had much less severe injuries than Clebe's, yet wanted to do nothing but sit around the house in bathrobes and watch TV all day, letting their families wait on them.

However, I didn't think I was prepared for Pike's Peak.

"Oh, Clebe, my legs are sore from yesterday's hiking. Aren't you tired?"

It was a dumb question. I knew the answer. My husband had always been a man who pushed himself to the limit, no less now with one eye and one arm. If anything, he has more to prove to himself now than ever. His reply didn't surprise me.

"No. Let's do it. It will be fun."

I wasn't about to let him go by himself. I wanted not only to talk myself into going, but also to convince him that I was happy too. Because, in a way, I was. He told me to just wear a pair of Bermudas and a T-shirt, but I also took a sweat shirt because I knew that the higher we climbed, the chillier it might get, middle of summer or not.

I wore track shoes and carried a tape recorder and some Psalms and Proverbs tapes, along with some music. About halfway up the mountain, I needed those music tapes. The climbing was steep, and the altitude made breathing difficult. I was spent, but knowing Clebe, there would be no turning back. One of the songs on the tape had lyrics that encouraged believers to "keep on believin' and don't quit. You might stumble and you might fall, but keep on believing if you can still crawl. And don't quit."*

I fell a little behind my marathon-running husband, who would one day set a treadmill world record for his age group at Kenneth Cooper's clinic in Dallas, Texas. I felt confident as Clebe looked back often so we wouldn't get separated. The next time he did, I was careful not to look miserable or ready to give up.

I called out to him, "Clebe, I'm thirsty."

"There's a cabin up ahead and a stream. We can stop there and get a drink."

I felt like we were on a trail in Vietnam and I was one of Clebe's troopers. Clebe loved to drink from any stream, but I always worried about contamination.

I'd seen the signs, too. I was surprised Clebe had, because he had ignored the ones that said: BEWARE. GO NO FARTHER.

*Mark Lowry, "Don't Quit."

Apparently there was a lot of snow on the top of Pike's Peak and no sense going on. At the cabin Clebe talked to a ranger.

"How much farther to the peak?"

"Quite a ways."

"Is it clear?"

"What? You mean the way to the top?"

Clebe nodded. I couldn't believe he was asking. Maybe he *hadn't* seen the signs. The ranger shook his head.

"Signs all over warnin' ya not to pass. No use to try. You can't get through up there. Snow. It's all sliding, slick, bad, a mess. Can't do it."

I knew that was the wrong thing to say to Clebe McClary. *Can't* is not in Clebe's vocabulary. Oh, he nodded and smiled to the ranger to indicate he had heard and understood, but I could see by the look on his face that this was just the challenge he loved. And that wherever he went, I was going, too. Clebe's father never let him say "I can't," and he doesn't let me or our girls say it either. He always says you can at least make an effort. Never simply decide that you can't.

He turned to me, "Honey, let's go as far as we can. We're going to see some territory we've never seen before."

I followed him, but I had a premonition that—like so many other ventures of ours that started out fun—this would end in frustration because of his daring. He likes to push himself to the edge of disaster, to test his endurance, his courage, his will power.

He coddled me by stopping for hugs and kisses every so often when we found secluded spots. As the afternoon wore on and it got cooler, the air grew thinner, and we neared the end of the tree line. We finished off our second to last soft drink and all our crackers, and I wondered why we hadn't simply driven up the beautiful paved road on the other side of the mountain. But to Clebe, that would have been no challenge, certainly no achievement.

We had been climbing steadily for more than ten hours when we finally rose above the tree line. I had enjoyed having trees all around because if I fell I would be able to grab a tree and suffer only scratches and scrapes. If I fell now, there would be nothing to grab. I was ready to call it a day and head back down, but that would have been almost as difficult for Clebe as continuing to climb. Going up with one arm and hand was a lot easier than getting down. Clebe's plan was to reach the gift shop and restaurant at the top and catch a ride on the train down the other side. Short of a calamity, there would be no turning back now. There I was in sweat shirt, shorts, and track shoes, and all around me were ice, snow, brilliant blue sky, and thin air. I feared the worst. Clebe, as usual, assumed the best.

"Dea, look how beautiful it is!"

I couldn't argue with that. The colors were rich and deep. It was still. But I couldn't see a trail. Neither could Clebe. He edged along from rock to rock, carefully moving up, hoping the snow under him lay over solid ground and didn't camouflage a crevice that would carry him to his death. He was farther and farther from what I guessed was the path, but he was determined to keep going. I followed him haltingly.

He moved to the edge of a clearing and looked straight down the mountain. We would have to backtrack. I stayed behind him several feet, but when he turned to come back, small stones under the snow gave way and he sat down. With only one hand to guide himself he tried to rise and ease his way back down, but he kept slipping. I wanted to get to him to help him, but he was coming faster and faster. There was no way to tell whether the ground beneath him was solid.

Clebe slid on his bottom the last several feet to where I stood, cutting his seat and the backs of his thighs on the rocks. That was the only way he could slow himself to keep from shooting past me and sliding back down the way we'd come.

"Clebe, this is ridiculous. We've got to get down."

He said nothing and led me up another way. This time the ground beneath him was clearly unstable. Some of it was snow, covering holes that led all the way down the mountain. Again I stayed back and beneath him by several feet, watching, wondering, hoping, praying. He took a few tentative steps and felt the snow begin to give way. He tried his foot in another direction. Still no good. Even the way he had gone up was not solid beneath him when he tried to reverse direction. I had a mind to leave him there. This time he couldn't get down by himself.

"Dea, you've gotta help me. I'm stuck on this ice ledge."

I was needed, but what could I do? And why did our fun times always have to end up like this?

"Clebe, when I get you off of there, we're turning back."

"We can't, Dea."

When Clebe said "can't," I realized we were in danger.

"We're going to, Clebe. I'm telling you. I've had it with this."

"Deanna, listen. We really can't go back down the way we came. It'll take longer in the dark, and we'll freeze to death. The shop at the top is our only hope. We have to make it up now. We're beyond the point of turning back."

I didn't want to hear that. I was getting a headache from the altitude, the blinding late afternoon sun, the chill, the fatigue, the effort, and the fear. Clebe stood on the ice afraid to move for fear of plunging through to his death. There was no way to tell if the ledge could hold him anywhere but right where he was standing. I headed straight back down to see if I could find a branch or twig to test the ground while I tried to get to him. I did a lot of heavy talking with the Lord.

"Please help us get out of this. I feel like I'm asking You for a lot of help for the stupid things we get ourselves into, but ol' hardheaded Clebe just had to keep going . . ."

I hadn't gotten far when I spotted a long, smooth branch on top of the snow that looked as if it had been placed there just for me. It almost looked like a carved tree or like Moses' staff. I struggled back to Clebe and used my staff to test the ground before me on each step as I edged out onto the ledge, poking it into deep drifts and crevices. It's a good thing I did. Once it went all the way through and kept me from falling into a gap. Finally, I got close enough to Clebe and reached across with the staff so he could grab the other end and slowly make his way down behind me.

Every time we saw a clearing, we thought we had reached an easier point. We were disappointed every time. Clebe would stop and predict that the worst was behind us, and he'd try to get me to agree how beautiful it was up there. But my head was pounding, and nothing would look good to me until we reached the top. How much farther could it be? Clebe could tell I was getting panicky.

"Look down, Dea."

"I can't look down."

"Then look up."

"I can't look up either. I can't look anywhere but straight ahead. My head is killing me. And I'm thirsty."

"Get out that last Pepsi."

Because of the altitude, the drink foamed all over when we popped it open. We drank a little of the foam, but it was hardly satisfying. And now we were out of food and liquid.

"Clebe, I'm really feeling weak."

He tried to motivate me. "C'mon, Dea, it can't be much farther. Let's keep movin'." As we hurried on, my head throbbing, we searched for a clear shot to the top. We turned a corner and faced a solid wall of ice, and we feared it was our only hope. That was the first and only time I ever saw Clebe's face turn ashen. Even he was scared. Then it was my turn to encourage him.

"Clebe, we can do it. We've come this far. We can do it. My staff is proof of that."

We carefully edged our way around the wall, praying we would pick up some semblance of a path. If there was no way around, we would have to go back down. I doubt we'd have survived the ordeal.

We had to go single file. What a relief to see a passable area and a slight curve to another clearing! When we got around that bend we came to a rough-hewn sign: THIRTEEN GOLDEN STEPS.

For an instant I was convinced that my staff had literally been thrown down from heaven by God and that He had etched that sign for us, too. I actually considered the possibility that this was a message to us that we had to climb just thirteen more steps and we'd be in heaven.

The only problem was that Clebe insisted I get rid of the staff. Only he didn't dignify it by calling it a staff.

"That stick's goin' to be in your way."

I reluctantly let it go, praying that God would provide it for some other troubled climber someday. Clebe was determined to make it now.

"Okay, honey, we've got to do it."

"Do what?"

"Go up this mountain."

"Tell me how!"

"Follow me. I'm going to kick in and make some places for you to step. You follow, and we'll take it slow."

"Let me go first, at least, Clebe. I can warm my hands when they get cold by rubbing one and hanging on with the other. What are you going to do when your hand turns blue?"

"I know what I'm doing, Dea. Let me do it."

The going was slow, and his hand indeed turned blue. When he could rest, he stuck his right hand under his left stump and warmed it briefly. Every step we took put us in danger of falling through the ice or sliding over the side. When we finally got to a spot where rocks jutted out, we held onto them for dear life, like they were islands in the middle of a flood. We said nothing. We just concentrated. And my head thundered.

After an hour of agonizing work, as the sun slipped under the horizon, we looked up to see what looked like a pink, new dawn. We knew better. We knew what time it was. But we heard a train, and we sensed a clearing was near. Were we on the right peak? Were the shop and restaurant nearby? Was that our train we heard? Would it still make another run this late?

We were so excited we had to talk ourselves into being careful until we had really reached the top. When we got to the lodge, which sat on a ridge several yards from the top, a dozen or so people applauded. They had been watching us through telescopes, and they could hardly believe we'd made it. Neither could we.

Clebe told me that because he knew I didn't feel good, he was going to try to get us a ride down the other side.

"I don't feel good? No, Clebe, I'm sick. Really sick."

I was the most relieved person in the world. While Clebe was off discovering that the train was not free after all, but that it would cost us several dollars each (I had a quarter on me), I trudged into the lodge and talked to the girl behind the counter.

"That was the hardest thing I've ever done in my life."

"What's that?"

"My husband and I just hiked up that wilderness trail."

"Really? How much equipment did you have to bring?"

"You're looking at it."

She stared at my shorts and sweat shirt, and she laughed. "What're you talkin' about? There's no way you got up that thing."

"We *did*. It was a miracle."

I didn't have the heart to tell her my husband had only one arm and one eye.

"I've lived here for years, and I've never tried hiking that trail. This is the worst time of year to do it, with the snow and ice melting and sliding."

"How well I know."

"Without ropes and equipment, it's a wonder you didn't fall into a crevice."

My only piece of equipment had been heaven-sent.

A few minutes later, when I went out to see how he was doing, Clebe was gone. My head hurt so bad that I decided that if anyone looked as if he were heading back down, I would ask for a ride. I thought the top of my head was going to blow off. The only person I saw near a car was an Indian with a turban. If he didn't speak English, I would use sign language. I had to get down off that mountain!

Next thing I knew, someone was calling. "Deanna? Deanna?"

"Yes! I'm Deanna!"

"Your husband was jogging down the mountain, looking for a ride for his sick wife. He found us. Have I found you?"

"You sure have."

By the time we caught up with Clebe, I was so sick I prayed the Lord would keep me from throwing up in this good Samaritan's car. The wind blew, and the car lurched from side to side. I was nauseated from the pain of the headache, so the trip down the mountain was almost as bad as the climb up. We wound around and around the mountain until I didn't think I could stand it anymore.

When we finally got back to our car, it was all I could do to thank the man, and then I didn't speak to Clebe all the way back. I wasn't angry with him—though I suppose I could have and should have been. I was simply in pain and could hardly move, let alone talk.

When we got back to the Hatfields, Ken ran out to the car and helped us into the house. I got into a tub of water as hot as I could stand it, took some aspirin, and considered the prices I paid to have a unique marriage. Only later did I find out how Ken knew to be so sensitive. Late in the day he had remembered Clebe's plan to hike Pike's Peak. When he called Sandy to tell her he was on his way home, he told her to pray for us. He knew the weather was terrible for a climb, and he also knew that Clebe would never hesitate or turn back. I believe their prayers saved our lives. (Maybe their prayers even sent the staff!)

A dinner outing was planned that night, but I couldn't go. All I wanted to do was stretch out in front of a fan and sleep. By then, of course, Clebe was feeling great. He is the healthiest, most in-shape, resilient person I know.

A couple of years later we were in Vail, Colorado, for a national floor convention where Clebe was a speaker, and he asked if I wanted to go hiking. I really didn't. If it weren't for him, I'd probably just sit around, relax, and read.

"Honey, I would really like to just stay in and take a nap or something. Why don't you take a nap with me?"

"Nah. I really feel like I need to get some exercise."

I couldn't let him get into too much better shape than I, so I reluctantly changed clothes, filled canteens, and agreed to go along. We walked and walked at Glacier Lake, and I fell farther and farther behind. After several hours, I yelled to Clebe, "When are we going to get there?"

He shrugged and kept plowing on, and I thought of the number of times over the years I had found myself in just that position. Getting there was worth it. Once we got where we were going, we would talk, really talk. Out in the middle of nature, where Clebe was most comfortable, he would talk like he never did in civilization. I could endure almost any difficulty, any drudgery, for that.

When we finally arrived at the beautiful crystal lake with the glacier around it, I was stunned to silence. Then Clebe and I praised God, thanking Him for His faithfulness and for allowing us the privilege of enjoying so many of His beautiful creations. The wind was cool as we ate our little lunch, and then we had the talk I had been waiting for, the one that was worth the sacrifice. Sure, there's always the temptation to stay at the hotel so I would be rested up to enjoy a nice dinner out with him, but women who settle for that are not willing to pay the price. They won't give what it takes.

The times I've made the effort have been the most rewarding in our marriage. After all these years, I still want to learn all I can about him. I ask about his childhood, his dreams, hopes, aspirations. At Vail I learned tons and was thrilled at how close we'd been. I felt so happy that we had hiked together, that I had made the decision to go.

Near the end of the trail on the way back, I stumbled and fell. I wasn't hurt, but I was tired, and I needed Clebe's strong arm to help me up. As he pulled me up, he brought his face close to mine.

"Dea, you know what? Of all the girls in the world, you're

the only one I've ever known who would be willin' to do something like this with me. Who else would be willin' to get grimy, tired, and sore with blisters all over your feet, yet never complain? You always go with me, and we have a great time. You're a great friend. And a great wife."

I would have hiked Pike's Peak again right then. Well, maybe the next day.

Epilogue

I hope our love story is a testimony to you, especially if you're struggling and hoping that one day your marriage may experience renewal. I can't begin to claim that Clebe and I have a perfect marriage, but it is special, especially in this day of rampant divorce. I firmly believe there is a special blessing on those who commit to love each other until death.

You may find yourself envying what we have. Warning! Danger! It's always easier to daydream about what could be rather than to tackle the situation at hand and remedy the corrosive spots in your own marriage. Just as rust can corrode a pipe and render it useless, so can the rusty areas of your marriage paralyze it.

The enemy lurks, trying to divide those who strive for God's ideal. What a feather in Satan's hat if he can ensnare dedicated couples! Clebe and I often face temptation. Every day we make choices that affect our future. We are not immune to temptation, but we know the danger of yielding to it. People try to wear down our moral principles by feeding us worldly garbage—the myth that everyone else is doing it, so why not you?

While Clebe was in Vietnam, he sent his men into a fenced area to retrieve a sign written in Vietnamese. He and the men knew they had discovered something exciting. In their haste they used little precaution, and upon reporting to base with the sign they learned through an interpreter that it read, "Danger! Mine field."

Every time we're lured into a situation we know is a dangerous mine field, we must remember that we not only risk our marriages, but we also risk the lives of those around us.

I love it when Clebe says, "Honey, you are the wind beneath my wings." Yet I can be to Clebe only what I allow God to be to me. I'm not always upbeat or an encourager. There are days I wake up grumpy, ill-natured, and resentful.

Clebe doesn't always brag on me. In fact, in spite of his chivalrous ways, he can sometimes make little remarks that make me feel like an utter failure. On days like that I can pity myself and mourn my plight in life, or I can return to the truth of God's Word in Romans 5:3–5 and Habbakuk 3:17–19. In spite of barrenness, wilderness, and famine, I can choose my attitudes. I can do what is right, even when it's easier to do the opposite.

After years of counseling and listening to women share their deepest hurts in marriage, I know there is no perfect marriage. But there is a perfect Savior. In spite of all the obstacles and challenges and unique demands placed upon us, we can choose to rejoice in the Lord, "I will joy in the God of my salvation, He is my strength."

Clebe and I have decided to get married again to celebrate our twenty-fifth wedding anniversary. We announced that in Clebe's movie (*Portrait of An American Hero,* Gospel Films), and people from all over the world have said they'd like to be there. Many say they want to do the same for their anniversaries.

This time we're really going to do it up big. We'll try to have everyone who was involved the first time, but it'll be great to have our daughters and new friends involved, too. I may hire a hundred photographers, just to make sure we get the pictures we want!

Clebe says that this time he's not going to be foolish: "I'm gonna kiss the bride!"

So many people miss the fun and friendship in their marriages. They have the license, the sex, the meals, and all that, but they never cultivate the friendship. They're missing the real delight. They vow they'll accept each other for better or for worse, but then they try to find the worst. I try to find out the best about Clebe, what makes him unique, what will make him grow. I search his history, his upbringing, to see what makes him so special.

We've truly become a team, and God has blessed us with the sensitivity to meet people at their deepest points of need. Often I sense where someone's most painful ache is—spiritual, physical, or emotional—and am led to minister to them with a word or a touch. Clebe has the perfect gift of being able to challenge people to press on regardless of their circumstances.

In spite of—in fact, because of—all we've been through since that traumatic day in Vietnam more than twenty years ago, I'm committed to love my husband. We have invested much time into our marriage and the dividends we receive now far outweigh the lean times. It's a lifetime commitment I've accepted with pleasure.

My commitment to love is my gift to God for His gift of life to me. May you view your commitment to love in a new light after reading this book.

ACKNOWLEDGMENTS

Apart from the commitment of Jerry Jenkins, Janet Thoma, Lori Quinn, Susan Salmon, and the others at Thomas Nelson, this book would never have been published. Your faithfulness, dedication, expertise, and sensitivity have helped focus me and direct me toward the completion of the book. Jerry, especially, thank you for your understanding and for being able to capture me on paper. To all of you, in your professional ability, you have not lost the personal touch I value so much.

It would take a couple of volumes to list you special friends who have a forever place of love in our hearts. Clebe's and my commitment to love has been especially blessed by our friendship with you and I wish to thank all of you, especially our parents, Dean and Caroline Fowler and Pat and Jessie McClary. May your commitment to love be an encouragement to others and your willingness to give what it takes, an example of hope to young men and women who need to know the transforming power of true love.

To my brother and sisters and their families—Dean and Gail Fowler (Trey, Melodygail, & Deanne); Dr. Joe and Annette Jemsek (John and JoAnne); Dr. Conyers and Jennie O'Bryan (Edward)—and to Clebe's sisters and their husbands—Norbert and Virginia Delatte; Billy and Patty Barron—you know that I love you.

Many thanks to our other family members and friends: Lucille Delavigne; Mary Vereen; Rosa McClary; Juliet Jones; James and Kat McClary; Col. Bill and Aida McClary; Nancy Hart; Jack and Estelle Fowler; Arthur and Alice Fowler; Sam and Jean Fowler; Clarence Edward and Belvagene Willis; Walter and Betty Willis; Randolph and Emily Ann Willis; Braxton and Virginia Lovette; Linda Simpson; Johnnie McClure; Art and Linda Chastain (Jason and David); Margaret O'Bryan; Ike and Sharon Bullard; Harold Morris; Diana Jenkins (Dallas, Chad, Michael); Radcliffe Cheston family; Coach Ken and Sandy Hatfield; Tim and Connie Foley; Pat and Mary Sue Lester; Tom Lester; Corey and Kay Wynn; Coach Fisher and LuAnn Deberry; Hatcher Story; our pastor, Bob and Lydia Barrows; Stewart and Rita Garrett; Jimmy and Pam Severance; Ed and Jean Cribb; Dr. Felix and Miriam Haynes; Dr. Richard and Harriet Furman (Ben, Tricia, Holly).

Deanna and Clebe McClary are committed to helping others overcome the tragedies and disappointments in life by sharing how Christ brought them through unbearable pain.

If you want more information or would like to secure Deanna or Clebe for a speaking engagement, you may contact them through their organization:

Clebe McClary, Inc.
P.O. Box 535
Pawleys Island, SC 29585
(803) 237-2582

Publications available through Clebe McClary, Inc.:

Living Proof—Clebe's biography.
Portrait of an American Hero—Movie by Gospel Films
    and Clebe's and Deanna's life.
Deanna's Testimony—Cassette Tape.
Clebe's Testimony—Cassette Tape.